BROKEN PROMISES, BLINDED DREAMS

Taking Charge of Your Destiny

REGGIE WHITE

Cover design by Kirk DouPonce, UDG/DesignWorks
www.udgdesignworks.com

Treasure House

An Imprint of

Destiny Image® Publishers, Inc.
P.O. Box 310
Shippensburg, PA 17257-0310

"For where your treasure is, there will your heart be also."
Matthew 6:21

ISBN 0-7684-3013-5

For Worldwide Distribution
Printed in the U.S.A.

This book and all other Destiny Image, Revival Press, MercyPlace,
Fresh Bread, Destiny Image Fiction, and Treasure House books
are available at Christian bookstores and distributors worldwide.

For a U.S. bookstore nearest you, call **1-800-722-6774**.
For more information on foreign distributors, call **717-532-3040**.
Or reach us on the Internet:
www.destinyimage.com

DEDICATION

I'd like to dedicate this book to all of those who came before us and paved the way to provide the freedom and ability to pursue our dreams: Jim Brown, Jackie Robinson, Deacon Jones, John Mackey, Kurt Flood, Marion Motley, Hank Aaron, Mohammed Ali, Bill Russell, Sidney Portier, Sojourner Truth, Dr. Martin Luther King, Jr., Frederic Douglas, George Washington Carver, and so many others. And to our forefathers of faith: Abraham, Isaac, and Jacob.

CONTENTS

FOREWORD

By J. C. Watts, Jr.

PLAYING QUARTERBACK AT EUFAULA HIGH SCHOOL and at the University of Oklahoma, I learned a lot about what makes life successful. Those years on the team were a proud and important chapter of my life. And becoming a part of that team reinforced many things I learned at home: hard work, sacrifice, commitment, to name a few. To a bunch of sports-loving kids, our coach was the high priest. He taught me that although I was the quarterback on the team, I had to live by the same set of rules as every other player. Sports today is much different than when I played 16 years ago.

Back then, few players earned the place in our young hearts that Reggie White continues to hold. He has a spirit of excellence in all he does. He's been an excellent football player, but Reggie's always been so much more. He continues to be an outspoken visionary for the time in which we live.

Broken Promises, Blinded Dreams reveals the Reggie White whom few of us have met. We've caught glimpses of his fiery faith and uncompromising voice in sound bites and snapshots taken amidst the hail of lights and publicity surrounding his career. But very few have known Reggie White the serious thinker, a man seeking real answers to the very tough issues challenging the black community and America as a whole.

With all of the courage of a football hero, Reggie boldly tackles the political challenges of our time. He does so with honesty, integrity, and candor. Football is a great teacher, and Reggie White has learned well. In my own life, playing sports taught me patience, teamwork, and the importance of understanding the opposition. It also taught me how to execute against the opposition.

Many of us in the black community realize that yesterday's promises often have been broken, and the dreams attained by a few have continued to elude the rest who've become blinded by disillusionment. I applaud Reggie White for having the courage to seek answers beyond the traditional political and religious solutions offered to the black community. And I agree with him that it is time to rethink outdated solutions that have not worked.

For instance, I've been outspoken in my criticism of the welfare system. Although many political leaders consider welfare an offering of the compassionate, I've challenged that assumption. I believe true compassion should be defined by how few people are on welfare. Why? Because it means that we've created a path to success for those willing to work for it. And there are many who are willing, as we have seen over the past 6 years.

Broken Promises, Blinded Dreams calls for a common sense approach to the issues facing Black America today. I agree with this approach, and personally have called for common sense to navigate welfare legislation. We shouldn't pay people not to work. Instead, we should make it more rewarding to work than not to work, and I submit to you that we should eliminate the taxes completely on the first several rungs of the ladder to do that. It's time that all Americans got a real slice of the American pie, instead of just a handout of leftovers and crumbs from the economic table.

Reggie challenges all Americans, red, yellow, brown, black, and white, to reach for more than social scraps and empty promises. He inspires us all to seek economic parity, political distinction, and genuine individuality.

To do so means rethinking the group identity that is often forced upon us as black Americans. Group identity in politics will always force or put pressure on members to think or vote a certain way. I have not forgotten that I have a right as an American to be an individual and disagree with liberal, conservative, black or white. Neither has Reggie White, despite the fact that intellectual independence and popular political ideology don't always mesh.

In order to become a truly independent thinker like Reggie, one must be bold enough to face an onslaught of political and personal attacks. In my own experience, I've seen that such attacks are often biased, hit-and-run rumors, unsubstantiated charges, and just plain old lies.

Real change for the better will come to the Black community as unfettered political thinkers accept the pressures of the front line. My father used to say, "Dogs don't bark at parked cars." You have to be doing something worthwhile to get attacked. In politics, the human thing that you want to do is to strike back, but I have always tried to be conscious of my Christian witness. Since I could never figure out a way to punch my attackers in the nose and not have it affect my credibility as a Believer, I've decided that the next best way to respond to my attackers is to succeed.

What impresses me most about Reggie White is his willingness to be a witness to what he believes, when he could have easily taken a smoother path. That's what makes him a trailblazer, and his book, *Broken Promises, Blinded Dreams*, a powerful tool for a fresh vision. Thinking black Americans are reconsidering old, outmoded loyalties, and outdated models of dealing with poverty and education despite the current demonization of Conservatives in the black community.

Nevertheless, I'm convinced that Reggie White is a prophet of change and a preacher of reason, and his words are among the harbingers of a new paradigm in the black community. Political change will take place when bold, uncompromising voices speak out for truth and stand up against long-held failed political assumptions and outdated modalities. It's for this reason that I'm excited about Reggie's new book, which promises to help lead the charge. In *Broken Promises, Blinded Dreams*, Reggie White has scored his greatest touchdown.

ACKNOWLEDGMENTS

Many thanks...

To my mother, Thema Collier, and my sister, Christy, and brother, Julius, I love you guys very much. To my grandmother, Mildred Dodds, you've been the strength of our family and I love you very much.

To my wife, Sara, who has been a pillar of support throughout the 18 years we've been married. And to my children, Jeremy and Jecolia, who've been two of the greatest kids a parent could have.

To Keith Johnson, one of my only strong supporters during my hard times.

To Phil and Bonita Pulido, who have been like family.

To Hardy and Amy Nickerson, who have also been like family.

To Wayne and Maria Dozier, who have been the best in-laws a man could have.

To the Klarner family, you're the best neighbors in the world, and we love you guys.

To Eugene and Gia Robinson, I value your friendship very much.

To Keith Jackson, thanks for being there when I needed you.

To Chris and Patrice Tillison, you guys are great cousins.

To Leonard Wheeler, you've been a great friend.

To Todd Scott, thanks for lending an ear.

To Greg and Bernita Malloy, you guys have been a great support, and we value your friendship.

To Michael and Trina Perry, we love you guys.

To Anthony and Renita Pleasent, you guys are great neighbors.

To Monte Judah, thanks for your wisdom.

To Danny Ben Gigi, you're a wonderful man, and thanks for teaching me Hebrew.

To Charles and Maria Copeland, I hope I've been the kind of son-in-law that has made you happy.

INTRODUCTION

The Black Wall Street Massacre

UNTIL VERY RECENTLY, it was a slice of American history that remained virtually unknown. It was 1921, in the dusty town of Tulsa, Oklahoma, where a small group of disenfranchised black Americans had created their own flourishing community. They named it Greenwood.

Greenwood was left alone, and its citizens kept to themselves. The quiet little community was geographically isolated from the rampant racism that marked the times. Free from the standard legislative tangle that bogged down other black neighborhoods throughout the country, holding the people in poverty and despair, the residents of Greenwood became increasingly wealthy. They turned 35 square blocks into a thriving little metropolis of numerous stores, two movie theaters, a bank, a hospital, a post office, libraries, schools, law offices, and even a bus system. As the wealth of the community's industrious black pioneers continued to increase, Greenwood earned a reputation among other black Americans as the "Black Wall Street."[1]

The success of Greenwood flew in the face of commonly accepted—and negative—stereotypes about black Americans. Who could look at this affluent little community and dispute the notion that when blacks were given an equal playing field, they could prosper and thrive just as whites did, if not better?

For those who knew about it, Greenwood was fast becoming a monument to the possibilities that blacks could enjoy when not road-blocked by systematic injustice. Black Wall Street was a celebration of achievement, a triumph the destroyed the heavy yoke of lies placed on the backs of black Americans in the early 1900s.

As the reputation of Greenwood grew among blacks, it also became increasingly known among whites as well—including the Ku Klux Klan. The delight Greenwood gave to blacks was equaled by the rage it evoked in the Klan.

On the morning of May 30, 1921, at the Drexel Building on Tulsa's segregated Main Street, Dick Rowland, a Negro shoeshiner, rode the elevator as he often did—but this time he was alone in the elevator car with Sarah Page, a white elevator operator. According to eyewitnesses, Page allegedly screamed and Rowland ran away as soon as the elevator stopped at the lobby. The whites nearby accused him of rape.

Rowland was caught later that same day, arrested, and incarcerated at the jail housed in the Tulsa County Courthouse. In a tirade that had continued for weeks prior to Rowland's arrest, the *Tulsa Tribune* had placed the blame for the city's problems squarely at the feet of the Greenwood community. The truth was that Tulsa's whites tended to be economically poorer than Greenwood's blacks, an unforgivable sin in the eyes of the Klan. Taking advantage of the whites' resentment, the newspaper basically announced —and encouraged—the lynching of Rowland in an article on the front page and an editorial under the inflammatory headline "To Lynch Negro Tonight."[2]

Not surprisingly, a mob of whites came after Rowland at the jail. At the same time, a group of black men from Greenwood came to the jail to try to protect him from the danger they knew he was in. A heated exchange between the two groups erupted into gunfire; several men were killed. Lacking the kind of firepower the whites toted, the men of Greenwood returned home.

What happened after that constitutes one of the most horrific pages in American history—a page so shameful that it was torn from many history books.

The Tulsa police looked over the lynch mob and immediately deputized hundreds of these angry whites. The fighting continued throughout the night as the whites moved into Greenwood. So many individual blazes were set that a wall of fire tore through Greenwood, destroying everything in its path. As the community burned, the whites continued their killing spree, looting stores and homes and setting fires in the process. Some of the "deputies"—who were ostensibly there for protection—poured kerosene on the nicest homes in Greenwood and stood around, watching them burn.

Eventually, the Oklahoma National Guard arrived to suppress the riot. But by then, less than twenty-four hours after Rowland's arrest, Black Wall Street was nothing but smoke and ash. It's been estimated that twelve hundred buildings were burned or looted—or both.

"The dead fell so thick in the streets that the National Guard was diverted from quelling the disturbance by the task of piling up corpses onto wagons and trucks," Brent Staples wrote more than 75 years later. Recently discovered records place the death toll as ranging from three hundred to possibly thousands.[3]

In what amounted to little more than a footnote to the bloodshed, Sarah Page refused to press charges against Rowland.

For all Americans, it was a nightmare—one of the bloodiest racially motivated crimes the country has experienced. For blacks who knew about it, it was the death of a dream. In the stench of the smoke that swirled into the hot Tulsa sky that day were the broken promises of human possibility. Obscured by those smoldering ashes lay the blinded dreams of success, achievement, affluence, prosperity, and the economic independence of black America.

It's to those broken promises and blinded dreams that I dedicate this book.

ENDNOTES

1. Brent Staples, "The Tulsa Race Riots," *The New York Times Magazine* (19 December 1999): www.ncsu.edu/park_scholarships/symposium/2000/riot.html

2. Ibid.

3. Ibid.

SECTION ONE

REVISITING THE DREAM

CHAPTER ONE

UNDERSTANDING OUR STRUGGLE

Historical Dreams

Yes, friend, my feet is real tired, but my soul is rested.
—Weary, elderly woman during the
Montgomery bus boycott

LATE ONE SUMMER AFTERNOON, Sara and I took our two children, Jeremy and Jecolia, to a rundown inner-city neighborhood where crime ran high and hope was in very short supply. We were participating in an outreach program and felt it was important for our kids to join us so they could see how other black American families live every day.

My daughter's eyes widened as we entered the tiny apartment of an elderly woman. There were no screens in her windows, and flies darted around in the stale, hot air. One noisy fan moved slowly, barely stirring the stifling heat. The sweet woman walked slowly into a tiny kitchen to make us a drink.

We left the apartment building and walked along a city street strewn with broken bottles, trash, and paper. A tiny boy with a runny nose, who seemed barely old enough to walk, played in the street by himself amidst broken glass and graffiti.

Sara and I said very little to our kids as we walked along. Jeremy and Jecolia were somber, not whispering a word as we passed broken buildings, shattered glass, and piles of refuse. After we pulled into our large driveway, they seemed relieved and jumped out of the car. Sara rattled around in the kitchen for a while and served one of her great meals, but the kids barely ate. Their quiet, reflective mood continued all evening.

Jeremy and Jecolia have grown up cushioned in the prosperity that comes from having a daddy who is an NFL football star. Shielded from the harsh realities of racial inequality and prejudice, they've never experienced what is a constant in the lives of other black American children.

According to government statistics, the economic disparities between black and white children remain the broadest dividing factor between the races. Jeremy and Jecolia are among some of the most fortunate; a shocking 39.9 percent of black children are poor, compared to 11.1 percent of white children.[1]

In addition, government census figures show that in 1999, the median net worth in households headed by older black people was $13,000 compared with $181,000 for older white people.[2] Those who consider racial inequality to be a thing of the past need to follow the money trail, because that is usually where the truth about an issue really lies.

Sara looked at me with those big eyes of hers. She didn't have to say a word; the look on her face told me that she felt the kids were "getting it." They were feeling the effects of the sting of the poverty and lack others experience every day. It was a hurt that could have been theirs so easily had they been less fortunate, less prosperous—less lucky.

Sara and I had decided to take them into that dilapidated neighborhood to expose them to harsh realities with which they must grapple for the rest of their lives. Because even if they are Reggie White's children, they also are black American children.

They've inherited a racial legacy that includes being the target of hatred they have not earned, exploitation they did not deserve, and guilt and shame for sins they did not commit. That legacy also includes struggle, triumph, dignity, endurance, and faith in a God who is greater than every force of evil.

Sara and I want our children to realize how blessed they are. They are two truly wonderful kids. But we would like them to also understand that there is another side to life than what they have experienced. We feel that they will be far more likely to make a difference among less fortunate people if they can identify with the historical and economic realities into which those people were born.

My challenge is to help my children understand the struggles of the past so that they won't take what they have for granted. Both my kids are older now than they were on that long-ago summer afternoon, and I'm still having a hard time imparting to them an understanding of how we grew up.

Although I wasn't raised in extreme poverty, I've had to work very hard to make sure that my kids have a better childhood than I did. My wife and I want them to know what struggles we went through. We want them to properly appreciate the things they are privileged to have.

I've told them, "Look, you don't understand what has happened in this country. You don't realize how I've put my life on the line every Sunday risking serious injury to make sure you could live well."

THOSE WHO HAVE GONE BEFORE

I also want my children to understand that Reggie White did not achieve success by his own efforts alone. It took a lot of hard work with a great deal of God's grace. In addition, many black people had to suffer many things to pave the way for my success as a black man in America. There was once a time when blacks were not even allowed to participate in professional sports.

As black Americans, we simply must understand our history. If we don't understand what our privileges and opportunities cost to those who walked before us, then we'll never truly appreciate our present accomplishments.

We must identify the privileges and challenges as a nation and as a people that are ours through the corporate wisdom of our shared experiences—both past and present. The Bible says, "Wisdom is better than jewels; and all desirable things can not compare with her" (Prov. 8:11 NASB). Again, "Acquire wisdom! Acquire understanding! Do no forsake her, and she will guard you; love her and she will watch over you…Prize her, and she will exalt you" (Prov. 4:5-6,8 NASB).

Gaining wisdom assures success in the challenges our generation must face. Genuinely understanding the burden and triumphs of our past is a first step to our future as individuals, and corporately as a community and a nation.

I continue to seek wisdom by exploring the past and examining the present, with my mind set on the future. It's time to go to the next level as a nation and as black Americans. We must expose those things that hinder our progress, uncover the weaknesses of our present assumptions, and embrace the power of our unique character and stunning achievement. I challenge you to reexamine old, corrupt alliances that have failed us. I am calling for a mandate to take the black American community and this nation back to the promise of a forgotten dream. That dream was so eloquently spoken by one who has gone on before us. He said:

Human progress never rolls in on wheels of inevitability; it comes through the tireless efforts of men willing to be co-workers with God, and without this hard work, time itself becomes an ally of the forces of social stagnation. We must use time creatively, in the knowledge that the time is always ripe to do right. Now is the time to make the real promise of democracy and transform our pending national elegy into a creative psalm of brotherhood. Now is the time to lift our national policy from the quicksand of racial injustice to the solid rock of human dignity.[3]

—Martin Luther King Jr.
Written to fellow clergymen on April 16, 1963,
from the Birmingham, Alabama, city jail.

Understanding the Struggle— The Importance of History

The children of Israel understood the importance of their history. For centuries they have handed down the story of how they overcame slavery in Egypt. After Joseph died, the Israelites insisted on carrying his bones on their backs as they left Egypt. They made an oath to Joseph, and 430 years later they kept that promise. They refused to forget their past.

If you cut yourself off from your own history you lose your identity. The black American community lost its history once through the horrors of slavery, and it must never allow that sense of alienation to surface again. Losing our historical identity damaged us as a people. It caused us to be assimilated into a European mindset that had no place for us and that despised our distinguishing qualities—qualities that make us uniquely who we are.

I'm not suggesting that all black people should try to dress or act like their African ancestors. However, we should cherish our history, identifying our own lives with the struggles and successes of our forefathers.

Martin Luther King Jr. put it this way: "The Negro is the child of two cultures—Africa and America. The problem is that in the search for wholeness all too many Negroes seek to embrace only one side of their natures. The American Negro is neither totally African nor totally Western. He is Afro-American, a true hybrid, a combination of two cultures."[4]

Many of us also have been cut off from our spiritual history. Much of the rich history and the spiritual wisdom and insight that came with that legacy have been lost because of our historical amnesia.

Few of us in the black community remember our heroes, those who paid a great price for many of our freedoms, privileges, and benefits. We need to make sure we keep alive the tales of great heroes such as George Washington Carver who, without reading books or sitting in a classroom, received knowledge directly from God that transformed the agrarian culture of his time.

Born a slave in 1864, Carver became a celebrated agronomist, scientist, and educator who produced more than four hundred different products from the peanut, potato, and pecan. In 1953, 10 years after his death, he became the first black scientist to be memorialized by the federal government. A statue was erected in his honor near his birthplace in Diamond, Missouri.[5]

Carver shared his secret to success with his students. In prayer, he drew closely enough to God to hear His secrets. Those secrets were revealed in his vast achievements: the many uses for the peanut, sweet potato, and soybean; nine medicines;

20 cosmetics; 12 animal feeds; dozens of dyes and paints; and synthetic cotton, plastic, and rubber.[6]

Carver is only one of many truly great black Americans whose lives made an enormous impact on the quality of life for us all. The Jews will not let their people forget the Holocaust. We too must remember our history, including all of its pain, struggles, heroes, faith, and triumphs. We must remember so that we never allow our people to be enslaved again, not mentally, physically, educationally, or economically. Like the Israelites, let us enter our Promised Land carrying with us the memory of those whose lives paved our way.

THOSE WHO PAID A PRICE

The black community has enjoyed the leadership of many fine politicians who have been genuinely committed to helping our community. But very few have had the unselfish commitment and focus of Dr. Martin Luther King Jr.

I believe King was a true prophet in his time, a straight-up militant whose radicalism was rooted in righteousness. He earned the respect of the nation—and even that of his enemies—for the way he handled himself in the midst of adversity.

THE DREAM

King grew up in the South under an oppressive, bigoted system of racial laws commonly known as Jim Crow laws, named after a black minstrel-show character. These laws were an overt expression of deep racial hatred. That hatred was the bitter inheritance of the dark stain of sin from an economic system that enriched a few but robbed the soul of the nation. Under the Jim Crow system, blacks and whites were separated in every respect, from drinking at different fountains, using different washrooms, riding in different sections of buses and trains, and visiting different recreational facilities and parks, to living in different communities.

Of this system, King said:

> Every parent at some time faces the problem of explaining the facts of life to his child. Just as inevitably, for the Negro parent, the moment comes when he must explain to his offspring the facts of segregation. My mother took me on her lap and began by telling me about slavery and how it had ended with the Civil War. She tried to explain the divided system of the South—the segregated schools, restaurants, theaters, housing; the white and colored signs on drinking fountains, waiting rooms, lavatories—as a social condition rather than a natural order. Then she said the words that almost every Negro hears before he can understand that injustice makes them necessary: "You are as good as anyone."[7]

To address the degrading laws and racial bigotry that blighted the nation's soul and grieved him to the depths of his being, King, as his father before him, refused to bow down to them. Inspired by Mohandas K. Gandhi's nonviolent message, King determined that he could confront this unjust system by appealing to his own people and the nation through a display of righteous love and irrefutable justice.

Following seminary training, King accepted a position at the Dexter Avenue Baptist Church parish in Montgomery, Alabama. Here he befriended the young Ralph Abernathy, pastor of the First Baptist Church, who would become a lifelong colleague in the Civil Rights movement.

Both ministers were deeply disturbed at the way the city of Montgomery operated its bus lines. Although 70 percent of its passengers were black, they were treated with contempt in openly demeaning displays of racism. The front seats were reserved for whites, even when empty, and the back seats were left for the blacks. If whites boarded and their section was filled, blacks in the rear were forced to give up their seats. Often, elderly black women would have to stand so that younger white males could sit in their seats.

Blacks also had to pay their fares at the front of the bus, then leave the bus and walk to the rear door to board again. Sometimes the buses would drive away while the feeble elderly struggled to get on. Worse still, bus drivers greeted black customers with racial epithets and slurs, and black men were called "boys" regardless of age.[8]

In March 1955, a 15-year-old black high school student named Claudette Colvin refused to give up her seat to a white passenger. She was handcuffed and carted off to jail. King sat on a civic board, which protested the treatment. Nevertheless, the young woman was convicted in court and given a suspended sentence.[9]

Indignant, King joined the Montgomery branch of the NAACP and in short order was elected to its executive committee. He decided it was time for him to use his calling, his commitment to nonviolence, and his dedication to the community to work for change.

Earlier that year, Rosa Parks had boarded a bus following a long day of exhausting work. The bus had been overcrowded, which forced her to take a seat right in front of the black section. After more whites boarded, the driver ordered her to give up her seat. Tired and disgusted, she refused.

That refusal prompted the NAACP to launch a boycott that crippled the bus company financially. King said, "You know, my friends, there comes a time when people get tired of being trampled over by the iron feet of oppression! We have no alternative but to protest."[10]

King's impassioned sermons sparked the conscience of a generation. The movements and marches he led ripped open the philosophical fabric of America and changed the heart of its people. His courage and selfless devotion inspired Civil Rights activities for the next 13 years.[11]

A biography written for The King Center in Atlanta puts it this way:

> Dr. King's concept of "somebodiness," which symbolized the celebration of human worth and the conquest of subjugation, gave black and poor people hope and a sense of dignity. His philosophy of nonviolent direct action, and his strategies for rational and non-destructive social change galvanized the conscience of this nation and reordered its priorities. His wisdom, his works, his actions, his commitment, and his dream for a new way of life are intertwined with the American experience.[12]

The Montgomery bus boycott and the marches that followed were the first steps toward tearing down a system of institutionalized hatred against the black race. Still, I don't believe we truly understand the breadth and scope of King's dream. His vision was much broader than the way we present it today.

King dreamed of a system of true equality, free from racial hatred, bigotry, and strife—a system that offered dignity and economic and educational opportunities to all races. His dream went beyond blacks and whites living together. He dreamed of brotherhood, Christian love, and genuine freedom, peace, and mutual respect for all people in this country. From a dark jail cell in Montgomery, he prayed that he would never accept anything less than the full scope of his inspired dream for the United States of America. He said:

> ...If I have said anything that understates the truth and indicates my having a patience that allows me to settle for anything less than brotherhood, I beg God to forgive me...[13]

ECONOMIC INTEGRATION

Many of us think of King in terms of his fight for school integration. But he didn't just fight for equality for blacks in education. He also fought for the economic integration of the black American culture into the mainstream of this nation's prosperity. Since the Civil Rights movement began, we've seen our schools become integrated, but the economic opportunities of many black Americans have fallen way behind. Black Americans have been in this country longer than most European groups. Yet economic laws and community sanctions have worked to impede our progress. Most of the nation's poor continue to be numbered among its black citizens.

For genuine equality to come to this nation we must see increased economic opportunities offered to black communities. This will happen when black people begin to take a proactive position and make these things happen for themselves within their own communities. We are not looking for a handout but simply an open door of opportunity to prove our own value.

As an athlete I've had an opportunity to make it, but there are still millions of other black people who have not gotten a fair chance in this country. The opportunities we seek may never fall into our laps. We need to say, "If society doesn't want to give us the opportunities, let's make the opportunities for ourselves."

I believe that we as a people must stop depending on others to help us advance. We must step out and start trusting in God to help us. Those of us who have become successful must not forget from where we came. Others before us paved the way for us, and we, too, must pave the way for those who will follow us.

THE CURSE OF FORGETFULNESS

A legend exists about black slaves who were forced to walk around a tree to make them forget their past. It was called the legacy of the tree of forgetfulness.

African captors were afraid that one day the slaves would remember their oppressors and return to take revenge upon them. Therefore, they forced men to circle the tree nine times and women seven times. Afterward, they were forced to make a vow to satan promising to forget their history, their past, and their places of origin so that they would never seek revenge against the tribal leaders who sold them into slavery.

Unfortunately, many in the black community still suffer from the forgetfulness that was a result of our forefathers' idolatry. As a people, we must arise from the stupor of forgetfulness and emerge from under the curses of the past.

DON'T FORGET YOUR ROOTS

The Alex Haley book *Roots* helped immensely in redirecting our focus by helping us remember our origins. But many black people continue to walk in historical amnesia. In the Bible, God warns us against forgetting our past. He tells us to rehearse our history to our children, to speak of it often, and to never forget the price that's been paid by others who have gone before of us.

Many in corporate America want to forget about this nation's history of slavery. They say, "Forget the past." I remember hearing a man on the radio say that two hundred million slaves died on the slave ships that came to America. The host corrected him, and chided, "I believe there was only about ten million." *Only* ten million? That's still more lives lost than in the Jewish Holocaust. Ten million lives is an unspeakable loss.

The reason I had the opportunity to succeed in sports was in part because of the price other athletes paid, men like Jim Brown and Jackie Robertson. These men walked courageously through a wall of racial hatred and social injustice, paving a path for me and others to follow. I've never had to endure what they suffered. No one has ever yelled "nigger" from the stands at me as I played. But some of our forerunners experienced threats against their lives simply because they were black.

It was their courage and faith that allowed me to do what I'm doing today. They had the fortitude necessary to fight for what they believed in until they won. We don't fully appreciate their struggles today, and we have failed to successfully build on the foundation they laid for us.

We, as a community, stand at the precipice of a new era. The time is right to take a giant stride forward, going to the next level of prosperity and autonomy. However, if we forget those who went before us, we will lose much. Our lives will forever be enriched by their sacrifices, and their struggle is our enduring legacy. We honor their sacrifices by continuing the work they started.

It's important that we look back at our historical dreams— the noble pursuits of our past. Let's never forget the heroes of our past, those who fought the great fight for us. Let's never forget those courageous individuals who blazed our trail. Let's make an oath not to enter the Promised Land of our corporate dream without cherishing the memory of the sacrifices they made.

ENDNOTES

1. www.childrensdefense.org/keyfacts2.html.

2. www.nih.gov.

3. Jim Haskins, *I Have a Dream* (Brookfield, CT: The Millbrook Press, 1992), pp. 68-69.

4. Coretta Scott King, *The Martin Luther King, Jr. Companion* (New York: St. Martin's Press, 1993), pp. 8-9.

5. Jessie Carney Smith, *Black Firsts* (Detroit, MI: Visible Ink Press, 1994), p .261.

6. www.store.conservativepetitions.com/product_info.php?products_id=87.

7. Haskins, p .17.

8. Jules Archer, *They Had a Dream* (New York: Viking, 1993), p. 129.

9. Ibid.

10. Ibid, 131.

11. The King Center; Biographical Outline of Dr. Martin Luther King, Jr.: www.thekingcenter.com/mlk/bio.html.

12. Ibid.

13. Haskins, pp. 68-69.

CHAPTER TWO

DEFERRED DREAMS, BLASTED HOPES

Political Promises

*I tried to talk to the nation about a dream that I had had,
and I must confess...I watched that dream turn into a
nightmare as I moved through the ghettos of the nation and
saw black brothers and sisters perishing on a lonely island of
poverty in the midst of a vast ocean of material wealth... Yes, I
am personally the victim of deferred dreams, of blasted hopes.*
—**Martin Luther King Jr.**

TEMPERATURES HIT RECORD LOWS in Little Rock, Arkansas, in September 1957. And nine black teenagers marched in the morning chill toward the icy glares awaiting them at the city's all-white Central High School.

Before the students could set foot inside the school, Arkansas governor Orval Faubus ordered the Arkansas National Guard to keep the black students out. In doing so, the governor challenged the U.S. government to enforce the Supreme Court's order to desegregate the school.[1] The order came as a result of the 1954 landmark case, *Brown vs. Board of Education* of Topeka, Kansas. A unanimous decision had determined that segregation in public schools was unconstitutional.[2]

In response to Faubus's order, President Dwight D. Eisenhower federalized the Arkansas National Guard, an action that placed the guard under his control as commander in chief. That gave Eisenhower the authority to order the National Guard to leave Little Rock and send in the army in its place. His intention was to use army troops to insure a peaceful transition from a segregated school to an integrated one.[3]

As the teens entered the school—to the sound of whites shouting "Go home, niggers!"— the nation's battle with integration began. It was the first time since the Civil War that U.S. military forces had entered a southern city to enforce national policy. Little Rock provided momentum to the efforts of Civil Rights leaders to end racial segregation.[4]

Waves of massive resistance would follow as segregationist legislatures cut off funds to school systems that had the temerity to integrate. Some states adopted amendments to their constitutions that required schools to shut down rather than desegregate. Efforts to move school integration forward were met with complete intransigence, unifying and steeling white resistance. Eventually, pockets of northern whites would step in and balance the equation. By the 1960s, the lack of progress toward the integration of public schools became one of the strongest arguments for the Civil Rights Act of 1964.[5] Nearly 50 years later, a different kind of segregation remains entrenched in our schools. In addition, many blacks and whites are surveying the effects of all the pain and effort and wondering if the benefits really outweighed the cost.

DISAPPOINTING RESULTS?

For the most part, integration is a failed policy. The promises it made to the community never materialized into reality.

Black parents hoped that their children would receive the educational advantages enjoyed by white children. They expected that once white and black children got to know one another, racial hatred would end. Black parents hoped that their youngsters, armed with an equal education, would enter life with equal opportunities in industry and higher education. Eventually, all that would translate into greater economic rewards and leadership privileges.

Black Americans hoped that both black and white children would leave the public school system on an equal educational footing and with a broader, more wholesome understanding of other people—and that educated black and white young people would enter adulthood with equal economic expectations.

Did the concept of integration keep its promises? Although polls suggest that as many as 75 percent of Americans, both blacks and whites, believe we should stay the course when it comes to our commitment to integration in this country, both blacks and whites are rethinking the issue.[6]

Yet statistics show that schools are becoming more segregated, and many black leaders are increasingly seeing that as a positive thing. According to the Northwest Regional Educational Laboratory, "In 1968, 77 percent of black students attended schools with less than 50 percent white enrollment; in 1972, after court-ordered busing, the figure dropped to nearly 64 percent and remained virtually the same through 1986. In 1994, it rose to 67 percent."[7]

LEVELING THE PLAYING FIELD

Just how much equality have we realized despite nearly a half-century of integration? I've had the opportunity of traveling the country and closely observing our school systems. Huge disparities between predominantly black and predominantly white schools continue to exist. You can't convince me that the education many inner-city kids are getting compares to the education that kids in the suburbs receive. We need to figure out what can be done to level the playing field as much as possible.

I recently spoke to kids in the Milwaukee school system. I made arrangements and visited about six schools, starting out in the inner city. From that inner-city school, we visited a school right outside the city limits, and finally ended up at a school in the suburbs. The differences among the schools were glaring.

Inner-city students lacked motivation; they acted as if they couldn't care less about getting an education. In the suburban school—and there were a lot of black kids in attendance—the entire student body was better educated. Students seemed very motivated and eager to learn. The educational systems in the suburban schools, including the facilities and teaching staffs, were far superior. Suburban kids enjoyed the use of the latest computer equipment, unlike the city kids. The kids outside the inner city were simply getting a better education.

Often when we hear politicians and public officials talk about fixing education, they're really just interested in fixing the educational system in the suburbs. When problems spill over into suburban schools, everyone takes notice and gets involved in creating solutions.

You'll recall that the high school shootings of the 1990s, including the shootings at Columbine, were a suburban phenomenon. Yet, school shootings, guns, violence, rage—such things have been ongoing issues at inner-city schools for years. But when suburban white schools started getting swept into the national trend toward violence, suddenly everything changed. Now, politicians were fully engaged and wanted to deal with the problem. They wanted to change gun laws and other related laws, because now white kids were being impacted.

Our society responds in a completely different way to tragic events in the black culture. Black and Hispanic kids shoot and kill each other in the inner city, but those shootings don't get the same degree of attention that white shootings in the suburbs do. If politicians want gun control, why haven't more of them made a concerted effort to get guns out of the hands of inner-city kids?

Shootings and rampant violence are tragic events in any neighborhood. It's a sad fact that America only seems to respond when the elite of our society experience such tragedies. I'm convinced that if we ignore the sufferings of the least among us, God will allow those same sufferings to be shared by the greatest among us!

The Civil Rights laws enacted over the past 50 years have done little to address the unequal dispensation of justice in different communities. Why is it that so little has changed in that time? If the powerful political leaders who purport to care so intensely about Civil Rights issues are genuinely committed to change, then why has so little change been realized?

American justice comes with a price tag; those who can pay expensive legal fees get justice, and those who cannot pay often do not receive justice. Statistics show that white-collar criminals tend to serve less time than blue-collar criminals.

Nevertheless, as a community we will never obtain greater justice for black Americans unless we are willing to use our resources to make a change. Blacks invest vast amounts of consumer dollars into the American economy. We need to begin using some of our own wealth to help provide equal justice for all of our people.

How Integration Failed the Black Community

Roy Brooks, Warren Distinguished Professor of Law at the University of San Diego, contends that attempts at integration in this country have failed blacks on several levels and will continue to do so. In his book, *Integration or Separation: A Strategy for Racial Equality,* Brooks notes that:

> blacks generally attended schools with whites in the 17th and 18th centuries in New England, but were verbally and physically mistreated by them. As a result, blacks [Brooks uses the term *African American* throughout] petitioned the Massachusetts Legislature in 1787 for an "African" school in Boston. This was rejected and black parents gradually pulled their children out of the public schools and sent them to private black schools—often held in a private home.

According to Brooks, public school integration promised two things: "to strengthen black identity (both personal and racial self-esteem) and to improve or equalize scholastic performance. He maintains that racial integration has failed on both counts."[8]

Research, Brooks added, proves that black children had higher esteem in segregated schools than in integrated ones, a fact first discovered by scholars A. James Gregor and Ernest van den Haag.[9]

Brooks argues that:

> ...black scholastic achievement has improved but that the improvement is minimal and that black kids often do better in *de facto* segregated schools...According to a Department of Education report on black scholastic achievement, "[b]etween 1978 and 1988,

black American 13-year-olds attending integrated schools had lower rates of increase in reading and math scores than did children of the same age in *de facto* segregated schools." As sociologist David J. Armour remarks… "Not only has mandatory desegregation failed to produce educational and social benefits for most minority children but also research shows it can lead to adverse consequences for some."

He believes that integration has demeaned blacks and made them dependent…His middle course is what he calls limited separation. This is not legally enforced segregation, but voluntary separation…The purpose is to create a nurturing environment where "dignity harms" from whites are not possible or at least lessened.[10]

WE ARE OUR GREATEST RESOURCE

The policies of integration have worn down one of our greatest treasures—the strength of our communities. Integration can be a great thing, and I am all for it when it serves the proper purpose. But in many ways integration caused the black community to become less unified. When blacks were living together, many communities thrived. The people within those communities thrived, too.

Willie Mays was a highly successful black man who continued to support the black community he came from. Mays never left his community, but instead he became a powerful influence for good there. Blacks historically enjoyed a strong sense of community and a strong identification within that community. Likewise, we depended on one another and supported one another within our communities. Integration came in and tore down our communities and fractured our identity, dislodging us from our roots.

Integration of housing and schools created an exodus of wealthier blacks to the suburbs, leaving urban communities abandoned. Black business owners and other influential leaders took with them vital human and material resources, a drain that eroded our neighborhoods even further.

Obviously I am not totally opposed to integration, because I live in an integrated neighborhood. My point is that in our quest for integration we must not forget about developing and enriching the communities that remain.

Boston minister Raymond Hammond is points out that "no black leader wants a return to 'legally mandated separate-but-equal.' Nor does he favor black nationalism. But he does think that a community works best economically, educationally, and socially if it stays together."[11]

Even conservative Supreme Court Justice Clarence Thomas supports single-race schools, because they promote the self-esteem of black students. Many conservative blacks, while continuing to endorse the ideal of integration, are now saying that affirmative action and busing do more harm than good. In 1984, author Charles Murray charged those government programs with robbing the black population of its initiative and replacing it with entitlement, thereby making blacks dependent on the government.[12]

Integration served a purpose in its time. However, it cannot take the black community to the next level economically. In his book *The Ordeal of Integration*, Orlando Patterson argues that government programs have helped many black Americans to join the economic mainstream, but those programs can't be expected to further expand the black middle class.

THE CONCEPT OF TOTAL INTEGRATION

It's in the economic arena that we as the black community have not found parity. I believe that this is the next level to which we must aspire. We must be willing to shed policies that are propping up a system whose solutions are flawed and out-dated and short-term. We need fresh, energized solutions for our current dilemmas.

Failed government programs and self-sabotaging attitudes will only impede our forward progress. Therefore, we must be constantly willing to rethink and reexamine the vehicles of our past success or lack thereof. Like the stages on a rocket, some government programs, political alliances, and community leaders may have been good for their time. They advanced us in our journey as a people. However, to enter into the Promised Land of prosperity and peace, we must carefully examine the usefulness of these vehicles to take us into the future.

Another political and economic vehicle inherited from the 1960s is affirmative action. Just how well has affirmative action worked?

AFFIRMATIVE ACTION

Some affirmative action programs have genuinely benefited blacks by helping them get a college education. If those programs had not existed, many blacks would not have received the opportunity. Yet the debate over affirmative action rages both inside and outside the black community. At its inception, affirmative action was a powerful tool used to break through the barriers placed against blacks in the workplace and in school admissions offices. Although many want to keep affirmative action in place, some contend that because racial barriers have

41

been broken, ongoing affirmative action is doing more harm than good because whites may be treated unfairly.

For those who want to undo affirmative action I have to ask this: What is wrong with a black kid getting a break, even if he doesn't deserve it? Lots of undeserving white kids have gotten their share of breaks. When I look back at our history, I see lots of kids who were denied opportunities at a time when white kids were given unfair advantages. I don't feel sorry for a white kid who may be passed over, because there have been plenty of black kids passed over for many decades. It's doubtful that the white kids who feel they are being treated unfairly ever experienced the struggles that our people had to go through.

I would like to see opportunities for blacks that go beyond getting into a particular school or job position. I would like to see black entrepreneurs find opportunities to own their own businesses and make a major impact on their communities. But affirmative action programs do little to provide opportunities for ownership. So, although many of these programs have been beneficial, they have provided limited solutions; neither have they kept pace with the times.

The black community spends vast sums of money. In addition, our internal resources of talent, intellect, skill, and other abilities are endless. We must begin to patronize our own communities, building up and strengthening our own resources. Too often our strength is depleted when our resources are used to empower and enrich others, while our own communities continue to decline.

Just take a look at the boardrooms and executive offices of many corporations. That's where you will find racial inequality. Far too many companies are only racially diverse at the lowest levels of employment. At the higher levels, the attitude found in those same companies echoes the plantation mentality that asserted, "You can work *for* me, but you can't work *with* me." Often the same businesses and schools that claim to be racially diverse have no minorities at the highest levels of power. At the helm of these businesses and schools are people who say they want reconciliation with blacks, which seems hypocritical to me.

In addition, some black leaders believe that including white women as a minority in affirmative action programs dilutes the original objectives of those programs. Whenever a white woman receives preference over a black man or woman, some blacks understandably see this as a failure of affirmative action programs, which were instituted to correct racial inequities.

These and other underlying issues of affirmative action in this country need to be reexamined.

THE UNDERLYING ISSUES OF AFFIRMATIVE ACTION

Although I do not consider myself either politically conservative or liberal, I do have many conservative views. However, I also believe that we as a people need to stop allowing any political party to use us.

Many liberals—blacks as well as whites—believe they "own" the black vote, but in reality they have often done very little to advance the true black agenda. We as a black community have been used as a voting bloc to swing votes to support issues that we don't believe in.

In addition, politicians often see affirmative action as a way of bringing blacks into the mainstream. But the underlying attitude of many of these leaders suggests that blacks do not have the intelligence to make the grade without the help of these programs. Where they exist, such condescending and patronizing attitudes are completely unacceptable.

I believe in excellence, and I've lived my life striving towards it. I also come from a people of excellence, with enormous intellect, wit, creativity, dignity, and wisdom. Never should we accept degrading assumptions about our people.

TAKING ANOTHER LOOK

It may be time to step back and reexamine our old assumptions, some of which have brought us broken promises and ongoing disappointments. The social agenda of the past 50 years has not always served us well. A half-century later our poverty levels are still the highest in the nation. Our middle class has grown, but our inner-city communities are more depressed than they were during the Great Depression. The number of black children being reared without fathers is higher now than it was when our people were slaves. Something continues to be very wrong.

It behooves us as a people to stop blindly accepting political answers from others—whether from the right or left. It's time for us all to take a second look at existing programs and long-held ideas. As a black community, we need to constantly reexamine these programs, alliances, and attitudes. We must ask ourselves these questions: Are they good for us as a people? Do they need to be changed or improved? Are they advancing someone else's agenda or our own? Are they outmoded or outdated? Are they producing the results we want? Will they take us to the next level?

The football uniform I wore in college probably no longer fits me, because over the past few decades my body has changed. Our community and nation have changed as well. What worked well for us 50 years ago may no longer fit. It's time to open the closet and reexamine our old garments; maybe it's time to make a change.

ENDNOTES

1. A Brief History of Civil Rights in the United States of America: www.blackamericans.com/LittleRock.htm.

2. Civil Rights Time Line: www.infoplease.com/spot/civilrightstimeline1.html.

3. A Brief History of Civil Rights in the United States of America: www.blackamericans.com/LittleRock.htm.

4. John Yemma, "the new segregation: Black community reexamining school busing," *The Boston Globe* (15 January 1997): www.boston.com/globe/nation/packages/rethinking_integration/day2print.htm.

5. A Brief History of Civil Rights in the United States of America: www.blackamericans.com/MassiveResistance.htm.

6. Yemma, www.boston.com/globe/nation/packages/rethinking_integration/day2print.htm.

7. "Blacks and Latinos Face Increasing Segregation in School," Northwest Regional Educational Laboratory: www.nwrel.org/cnorse/infoline/may97/article2.html.

8. "Why Not Limited Separation?" Roy L. Brooks, *Integration or Separation: A Strategy for Racial Equality* (Cambridge, MA: Harvard University Press, 1996); reviewed by Louis Andrews (Vol. 1, No. 2, April 1997): www.lrainc.com/swtaboo/library/lra_is.html.

9. Brooks, www.lrainc.com/swtaboo/library/lra_is.html.

10. Ibid.

11. Yemma, www.boston.com/globe/nation/packages/rethinking_integration/day2print.htm.

12. Franklin Foer, "Racial Integration" (Slate MSN; 23 November 1997): www.slate.msn.com/id/1080/.

SECTION TWO

THE OBSTACLES AND CHALLENGES: WHAT WENT WRONG?

CHAPTER THREE

WHO'S MINDING THE STORE?

Civil Rights Leaders

A man who won't die for something is not fit to live.
—Martin Luther King Jr.

THE CIVIL RIGHTS MOVEMENT was in its infancy in the late summer of 1958 when Martin Luther King Jr. published his first book, *Stride Toward Freedom.* To promote the new release, he went to Blumstein's department store in Harlem to autograph copies. While signing books, a deranged woman stabbed him with a letter opener. Upon her arrest, she railed that King was a communist.

King's brush with death brought to the surface thoughts about one of his philosophical heroes: Gandhi. The leader from India had brought an end to British rule in his country through a sustained and altruistic display of nonviolent resistance. King had long dreamed of traveling there to survey Gandhi's accomplishments for himself. Following the stabbing he decided to make the trip. Afterwards, he said:

> The trip had a great impact on me personally. It was wonderful to be in Gandhi's land, to talk with his son...and to see the countless memorials for him....I left India more convinced than ever before that nonviolent

resistance is the most potent weapon available to oppressed people in their struggle for freedom.

It was a marvelous thing to see the amazing results of a nonviolent campaign. The aftermath of hatred and bitterness that usually follows a violent campaign was nowhere found in India. Today a mutual friendship based on complete equality exists between the Indian and British people...

The way of acquiescence leads to moral and spiritual suicide. The way of violence leads to bitterness in the survivors and brutality in the destroyers. But the way of nonviolence leads to redemption and the creation of the beloved community.[1]

King's commitment to nonviolence highlighted the purity of his purpose. He dreamed of brotherhood and peace between the races. One wonders what he would think about how his legacy has been handed down by those who have continued to run with his torch.

We need to reexamine the impact of today's Civil Rights leaders. How effective have their methods been in achieving the goals of civic equality and economic justice in the black community? Also, how effective have they been personally? Let's dig a little deeper to see who's been minding the store.

KING AND THE SOUTHERN CHRISTIAN LEADERSHIP CONFERENCE

Many Civil Rights leaders who speak for the black community are widely recognized and nationally acclaimed. However, I contend that unless a leader has been appointed by God, as was Dr. King, he is not a leader or spokesperson at all. Genuine leaders are not self-appointed, and they do not advance their personal agendas. Genuine, God-appointed leaders build up God's kingdom through God's divine enabling. Genuine leaders are servants of the people, not served by the people. Genuine leaders are those who are divinely empowered to make a difference in the world for good.

Too many of today's Civil Rights leaders are self-appointed men who appear more committed to personal gain than to the good of the community and country at large. The church has also fallen into that same practice of empowering its leaders but not its people.

Some in the black caucus often uses blacks and black issues as pawns to advance its agenda. Some leaders are empowered and enriched, but the black community as a whole is left feeling fleeced.

SELF-EMPOWERMENT, SELF-PROTECTION, AND SELF-AGGRANDIZEMENT

King wasn't always considered the leader of the Civil Rights movement. In fact, initially he didn't project himself as such. Nevertheless, he was divinely appointed to the hour in which he lived, and it wasn't long before many people acknowledged it.

We've grown up accepting the Civil Rights leaders who worked with Dr. King because of our love for him. But not all of these leaders embraced his heart and his priorities. Many of those involved with the movement became jealous of him. Consequently, many of those who were with him were really not *with* him. After he died, those leaders didn't continue to pursue the agenda he had established.

Trouble within the rank and file of the Civil Rights movement began to surface as the movement gained momentum and recognition. In the years prior to his death, King grew suspicious and impatient with the behavior of some of his staffers. He enlisted the help of European businessman and black Chicago native William A. Rutherford to help him address this matter, which resulted in resentment toward King.

> King outlined the problems to Rutherford in the presence of only King's most intimate confidants—Abernathy, [Andrew] Young, and Dorothy Cotton. "Martin said to me," Rutherford recalled, " 'Bill, there are two things I want you to do at the outset.' " The first concerned two SCLC staffers whose spending habits King found questionable. " 'Jim Harrison and Hosea Williams have an apartment at the University Plaza apartment complex,' " King told Rutherford. " 'How the hell can they on their salaries maintain a separate apartment,' " in addition to their homes? Neither King nor his colleagues suspected Harrison's mercenary involvement as a paid FBI informant, but King did wonder about his behavior as comptroller and why he could carry on an expensive lifestyle.

> King's other mission…"He said, 'The second thing I want you to do is, Jesse Jackson's so independent, I either want him in SCLC or out—you go whichever way you want to…' "[2]

Although Jesse Jackson was widely seen by the media as King's heir and right-hand man, that position was largely self-proclaimed, according to SCLC staffers closest to King. Rutherford wrote,

> Jackson was viewed as "an outsider and an undependable, egotistical self-promoter by many SCLC staffers."[3] Much of the trouble stemmed from distrust

of Jackson's personal motives. King's Chicago confidant Chauncey Eskridge explained, "I don't think we cared much for him." One former SCLC executive recalled, "He used to tell Jesse, 'Jesse, you have no love.' "[4]

Rutherford appreciated that King's unhappiness with Jackson went beyond spirit and ideology. "He didn't trust Jesse, he didn't even like Jesse. If you ask me if there was any suspicion about Jesse's motives and even devotion to the movement, I would say categorically yes there was—considerable. And we talked about it."[5]

KING'S RIGHT-HAND MAN?

On April 5, 1968, just 12 hours after an assassin's bullet killed King on the balcony of the Lorraine Motel in Memphis, Jackson announced on the NBC *Today Show* that King had "died in my arms." He recounted the story of how he cradled the fallen leader's head and was the "last person on earth" to whom King had spoken. As proof, he appeared on TV wearing an olive-brown turtleneck sweater that he claimed bore the stains of King's blood.[6]

The story made for enthralling television, and later that day Jackson appeared in public again, still wearing the bloody sweater at a public session of the Chicago City Council convened by Mayor Richard Daley to commemorate King. Jackson said, "This blood is on the chest and hands of those who would not have welcomed him here yesterday. He went through, literally, a crucifixion. I was there. And I'll be there for the resurrection."[7]

The story of King's last moments with his "heir," Jesse Jackson, was repeated four days later in the black-owned weekly newspaper, the *Chicago Defender*, and in more than a hundred times in news clips for the next seven years. An interview in *Playboy* in November 1969 called Jackson the "fiery heir apparent to Martin Luther King." Adding, "The Reverend Jackson's first national exposure came as a result of his closeness to Dr. King. He was talking to King on the porch of the Lorraine Motel in Memphis when the fatal shot was fired, and cradled the dying man in his arms."[8]

The story of King's dying moments with Jackson catapulted him to national prominence. Nevertheless, the entire story was a boldface lie. It never happened. The only person who cradled the dying leader was his closest friend and confidant, Ralph Abernathy, according to Hosea Williams, who was present during the shooting. "It's a helluva thing to capitalize on a man's death, especially one you professed to love," Abernathy said.[9]

Jackson was nowhere near the scene and disappeared shortly after the shots were fired, according to eyewitness reports. Photos taken following the shooting verify that Jackson was not there.

Since that much-heralded account, Jackson has successfully proclaimed himself as the rightful heir to King's legacy. He has built a world-class reputation as a leader of the black community. He has used the good will and honor that King paid so dearly for to position himself before presidents and world leaders and in corporate boardrooms throughout the nation and the world.

What has the black community received in return? Shockingly little. According to author Kenneth R. Timmerman, Jackson has threatened government and corporate leaders with boycotts and demonstrations in an effort that has netted him and his close friends and family billions of dollars. Yet the black community at large has seen little to none of that capital.

Shelby Steele, an black American scholar at the Hoover Institution at Stanford University, has called Jackson an "extortion artist for the grievance elite." He charges that Jackson's biggest failing was to have corrupted race relations in America.

National Center for Neighborhood Enterprise head Robert Woodson says Jackson's tactics don't benefit the black community; they benefit Jackson. "He uses the black community to threaten corporations, but then who benefits? It's not the black community. It's a handful of black businessmen around Jesse Jackson. What it's really doing is diluting the rich legacy of the Civil Rights movement. That legacy is now for sale."[10]

Black syndicated columnist Deroy Murdock believes that Jackson could be a great force for good if he would help black teens or black entrepreneurs instead of just helping his friends. "Jesse Jackson runs a black enrichment and fraud operation that benefits himself, his spider web of organizations, his business associates, and his relatives," Murdock has said.[11]

Jackson has been highly vocal about many issues in the black community, and he is seen as a champion of poor, disenfranchised blacks. But how well deserved is that distinction?

WHY THE SILENCE?

While extremely vocal about the evils of the slavery of the past, Jesse Jackson remains strangely silent regarding the ongoing practice of modern-day slavery. But why? Darrell Dumas, a black columnist and commentator, challenges Jackson to weigh in on the issue of the modern enslavement of blacks in Arab countries.

Responding to an article by Walter E. Williams detailing the black slave trade in West Africa, Dumas challenges Jackson's silence. Not only has Jackson "not fought against the slavery of blacks in slave trading countries, he has not even mentioned their plight," said Dumas.[12]

Jackson, together with the left-wing media, is strangely silent on contemporary slavery. Nevertheless, the slave trading of Christian blacks—especially black children—by Islamic blacks is at an all-time high.

Estimates of human slaves being traded by Muslims vary, but the numbers are staggering. Jay Williams, who traveled to Sudan as part of a contingent buying the freedom of 4,400 slaves there, said one source estimates that there are 27 million people enslaved worldwide.[13]

Other estimates are much higher. Anti-Slavery International, which calls itself the world's oldest human rights organization, claims there are currently 200 million people in bondage today. These, it argues, are not children paid poor wages working in inhumane conditions, but modern-day slaves who are shackled and held at gunpoint.[14]

So why *is* Jackson so silent on the issue of modern black slavery?

To answer that question, we need to look no further than Jackson's political affiliations. According to author Kenneth R. Timmerman, Muslim Arabs have been funding Jackson's organizations for many years. He said,

> Among the new supporters who attended the meeting were representatives of the League of Arab States, the Arab-American Congress for Palestine, the Palestine Human Rights Campaign, and the Libyan Embassy, according to the *Christian Science Monitor*. They immediately gave cash to Jackson's PUSH foundation, using

the banner of Arab-American University Graduates to pay for his new Middle East venture.[15]

Timmerman claims that Arab League funds "accounted for 80 percent of the money the PUSH Foundation had raised" during one year that Jackson was campaigning for the presidency.[16]

It's not that Jackson lacks the funds and the platform to fight this horrendous racial injustice against black children. He has enjoyed wide access to funds for just that purpose. But critics suggest that Jackson has used racial issues to enrich himself and has failed when it comes to defending the needy against racially motivated crimes.

I have a problem with anyone, whether it be Jesse Jackson or any other leader, taking resources and putting them into building their own organization instead of investing them into building the community. And Jackson isn't the only Civil Rights leader who is currently under intense scrutiny for using race issues to build his own extravagant empire.

VOTING ISSUES

Far too often black Democrats try to get people to vote, but they don't speak to them enough about the issues. Many of our people died for the right to vote, and we need to vote. But what good is voting if you don't know the issues? Many of our leaders patronize our people, pressuring them to vote without fully explaining their platform. Or even worse, they present only one side of an issue. Republicans, on the other hand, are perceived as ignoring the black community.

It's time for the black community to stop allowing our own people and others to use us as political pawns to advance everyone's agenda but our own. It's time we stopped allowing ourselves to be patronized and used. It's time our own communities started benefiting from our power to vote. Blacks represent a powerful voting bloc with great political clout. Many politicians understand that all too well. It's time that we recognized our political power and started using it to our advantage.

No More Excuses

Often the political agendas advanced in the black community do not empower the people by affirming their own internal resources. Instead, patronizing politicians create within blacks a self-image of powerlessness and dependency. The time for enduring this kind of condescension and demeaning patronage is over.

Many people have experienced legitimate struggles and injustices in the corporate world; highly qualified black men and women frequently don't get the positions they want in a company because of racial prejudice. Some black people sit back and say, "The white man is holding me back." Well, he can't hold you back if you do what you are supposed to do. Even if things are ten times worse because of the color of our skin, "If God is for us, who can be against us?" (Rom. 8:31 NKJV); successful blacks—especially those who trust God—refuse to make excuses about being held back in life.

Ultimately, nobody can hold you back unless you let them. I know men who experienced racial prejudice in just about every company for which they worked. They responded by becoming entrepreneurs and starting their own companies where they could call the shots. Eventually they made it on their own terms instead of accepting everyone else's terms.

We must take responsibility for our actions and learn how to succeed on God's terms; it's time we stopped living for anyone but God. When I do what God tells me to do, then no one can stand in my way. God will make a way for me where there seemingly is no way. I don't need to become a slave to someone else's agenda when I've got the God of Abraham, Isaac, and Jacob working on my behalf.

ABORTION AND PLANNED PARENTHOOD

One of the most blatant examples of the way liberal Civil Rights leaders have used blacks to promote their own agenda is the abortion issue. Historically the black community did not support abortion and did not believe in it; it's an agenda that is ultimately destructive to our people.

Abortion contributes to the disintegration of black families in this country. More young black women receive abortions than any other ethnic group. The black vote has made Planned Parenthood founder Margaret Sanger into a hero. But this woman hated black people. It is a well known fact that this woman made it her mission to eliminate blacks, Jews, and Catholics. Tragically, our vote has empowered and encouraged her agenda in our own communities.

Huge amounts of federal money pour into Planned Parenthood. When our leaders come into our communities and pressure us to vote in a certain way on the abortion issue without fully informing us, they are using us to help support Planned Parenthood.

ABORTION AND IRRESPONSIBLE SEX

A true community values its children, but we don't value children the way we should in our American culture. That's why it's so easy for us to abort them. Young people turn quickly to abortion as the solution when irresponsible sex gets them into trouble. They want the pleasure of sex without the consequence of responsibility.

When the rich young ruler asked Yeshua how he could obtain eternal life, He said, "If you want to enter life, obey the commandments" (Matt. 19:17b NIV). That statement is no less true today. The command that "thou shalt not kill" has never changed. Rejecting God's commands will bring curses on our lives and our communities.

When God gave the Ten Commandments, He warned: "This day I call heaven and earth as witnesses against you that I have set before you life and death, blessings and curses. Now choose life, so that you and your children may live" (Deut. 30:19 NIV). Today, we can see curses all around us—poverty, disease, pain, crime, death—and sometimes we wonder why. Let's never allow ourselves to become facilitators of the painful consequences of national sin by opening the door to sin through our votes.

SELLING OUT

It often seems as if some of our black politicians have been bought off. Many black political and religious leaders started off with a moral stance against abortion and other ethical issues, but now these same leaders support the issues they once opposed. They have sold out.

Compromising one's principles is a dangerous thing. It's an extremely serious problem when godly leaders sell out to someone else's political agenda for the good of a particular political party. That's how good leadership becomes corrupted.

Although most blacks are registered Democrats, they tend to be conservative thinkers when it comes to issues of morality. At the same time, most black voters elect liberal-thinking

Democrats who support issues that many of us consider immoral. Therefore, we often support a party that doesn't represent us as a people.

Most blacks vote Democratic purely because of tradition. In the past, Democrats catered to the black community through their support of affirmative action and welfare, and Republicans lacked sensitivity towards the issues that affect blacks. Therefore, many blacks feel the Democratic Party is the one willing to do the most for the black community. But Democrats have also hurt the black community by buying it off with irresponsible liberal thinking programs that keep blacks in an inferior state.

BECOMING WISE VOTERS

The black community is doubtless one of the most cohesive groups in this country. Our unity makes us an easy target for liberals when counting up their votes. They expect us to vote for them, regardless of their policies and overall agenda. They expect us to continue to be bought off with a few goodies, but they don't truly see us as equal political partners.

Too many of us in the black community, and the white community as well, see a lot of immoral things going on, but we remain silent. Consequently, sin flows unabated into our communities and into our lives.

The groups promoting immorality benefit from it financially, far more than the black community does. When a black individual finally does speak out, he or she comes under such a vicious attack from the media that blacks end up ostracizing that courageous person.

As believers, we must be compassionate, but we must never surrender our biblical values. There have been times when the media has attempted to suggest that Reggie White is a bigot because I disagree with a sinful lifestyle. I may be a Believer, but that doesn't mean that I should embrace the lifestyle of a child molester or any other immoral person.

The Messiah fought for the oppressed and the sinner, but He did not support their sin. He would have opened the door to the kingdom of God to any repentant person—homosexual, adulterer, black, white, rich, or poor. But He never would have carried a picket sign to fight for gay rights. Never would He have fought for the right of someone to commit adultery.

When religious zealots brought an adulterous woman to Him, the Messiah freely offered her forgiveness and love. But He did not give her permission to sin. He told her, "Neither do I condemn thee: go, and sin no more" (John 8:11b KJV).

Recently, my nephew was in a class in which the teacher was supposed to be discussing government. But the teacher started talking about homosexuality, despite the fact that it had little to do with the subject.

In an attempt to defend what he believes, my nephew came home and searched the Scriptures to prove that the teacher's views on homosexuality were wrong. All too often, parents are not even aware of what's being imparted into the fertile soils of their children's minds and hearts. The public schools are notorious for advancing liberal ideas, and often the parents are the last to know about it.

I have a problem with those whom I consider to be immoral trying to force their agenda on the rest of us through public policy or public schools. I share my personal beliefs and values with others, but I never force anyone to convert if they disagree with my faith. Why should our children be forced to accept the gay agenda through the curriculum taught in the public schools?

This is one of the reasons why I agree with vouchers and school choice. These programs provide parents with the opportunity to make a choice. Through vouchers, parents can veto the immorality that is being taught by various political groups.

A Political Agenda of Our Own

Instead of being used by a system that considers black voters as an easy avenue for advancing their own immoral, unethical, and selfish agendas, we as a community need to develop our own political agenda. We don't owe liberals anything for their help in the past. The objectives of the left during the Civil Rights era are very different from those of today. We must become more discriminating as voters, choosing our own objectives and goals in order to advance our own communities. We must become wise enough to discern when our own leaders have sold out and are no longer working for us.

Creating our own political agenda and choosing our leaders based on merit and not on hype and showmanship is part of the wisdom that we will need to advance to the next level as a community. It may take some stretching and some soul-searching, but I'm convinced that we have what it takes to succeed.

Not only do we need to carefully consider the political leaders and alliances we support, we must be ready and willing to reexamine our religious leadership as well. Let's take a deeper look at church leadership.

Endnotes

1. Jim Haskins, *I Have a Dream* (Brookfield, CT: The Millbrook Press, 1992), pp. 53-55.

2. David J. Garrow, *Bearing the Cross: Martin Luther King, Jr., and the Southern Christian Leadership Conference* (New York: William Morrow and Company, 1986), p. 584.

3. Ibid., p. 585.

4. Ibid., p. 584.

5. Ibid., pp. 584-585.

6. Kenneth R. Timmerman, *Shakedown* (Washington, DC: Regnery Publishing, 2002), p. 6.

7. Ibid.

8. Ibid.

9. Ibid., p. 7.

10. Ibid., pp. 340-341.

11. Ibid., p. 348.

12. Walter E. Williams, "The Slave Trade Is Alive and Well" (3 January 2001): www.darrelldumas.com/wednesday.htm.

13. Alvin Powell, "Slavery, Though Outlawed, Persists," *Harvard University Gazette* (15 November 2001): www.news.Harvard.edu/gazette/2001/11.15/06-slavery.html.

14. Ricco Villanueva Siasoco, "Modern Slavery," Family Education Network (18 April 2001): www.factmonster.com/spot/slavery1.html.

15. Timmerman, p. 109.

16. Ibid., p. 119.

CHAPTER FOUR

MISSING THE MARK

Church Leadership

The church must be reminded that it is not the master or the servant of the state, but rather the conscience of the state. It must be the guide and the critic of the state, and never its tool.
—Martin Luther King Jr.

SOME PEOPLE THINK I'M BRASH, bold, and overly opinionated about my faith. I'm not afraid to say what I believe. Martin Luther King Jr. once said that a man who won't die for something is not fit to live. I believe that. What a man believes will be tested, and standing tall when you're challenged is a mark of manhood.

A while back, a player from another team seemed determined to test my faith. We got along well enough when we played pro ball together, but he was constantly challenging my moral stand. He would curse and make comments about my faith to see if I would back down. At times, his nasty comments really tested my patience, although I always knew that he respected me as a player.

This player was on the opposing team in my final game. The media surrounded me, shoving microphones into my face and barking questions about my plans for the future. Meanwhile, from the corner of my eye I realized that other players were standing nearby waiting for me to finish speaking to the media. Usually the guys don't do that. Generally, they just say, "Hey, good game!" and go their way. The brother who had tested me over and over again was standing there among them waiting patiently.

Afterwards, I walked over to him, shook his hand, and hugged him. He gave me a big bear hug and made a surprising comment. He said, "I want to let you know that I respect you. You've stood up before people and said what you believed, and you've never let them back you down. I really respect you for that."

MARTIN LUTHER KING JR.—A MAN OF GREAT COURAGE

When someone makes a statement like that, what that person is really saying is he thinks you're a man. To be able to stand up for what you believe and not let anybody back you down is part of what manhood is all about. That's one of the reasons I respect Martin Luther King Jr. so much. He stood tall for what he believed, even when staring into the face of death. He was a great man.

Just hours before he was killed, he spoke these words:

I left Atlanta this morning, and as we got started on the plane, there were six of us, the pilot said over the public address system "We are sorry for the delay, but we have Dr. Martin Luther King on the plane." And to be sure that all of the bags were checked, and to be sure that nothing would be wrong with the plane, we had to check out everything. And the plane was protected and guarded all night.

And then I got into Memphis. And some began to talk about threats that were out. They asked what would happen to me from some of our sick white brothers?

Well, I don't know what will happen now. We've got some difficult days ahead. But it doesn't matter with me now, because I've been to the mountaintop. And I don't mind. Like anybody, I would like to live a long life. Longevity has its place. But I'm not concerned about that now. I just want to do God's will. And He's allowed me to go up the mountain. And I've looked over. And I've seen the Promised Land. I may not get there with you. But I want you to know tonight that we as a people will get to the Promised Land. And I'm happy tonight. I'm not worried about anything. I'm not fearing any man. Mine eyes have seen the glory of the coming of the Lord.[1]

The following evening King was shot and killed by an assassin's bullet. He never backed down, never flinched, never cowered. He boldly, courageously faced his own death to bring freedom and dignity to his people.

TAKING A STAND

Many leaders compromise their convictions out of fear that speaking out will cause them to lose opportunities, raises, contracts, and financial benefits. I'd rather say what I really believe and lose an opportunity than to walk away feeling ashamed because I was afraid to stand up. I've lost a substantial amount of money, along with endorsements, when I've spoken out on certain issues in the past, but I can't turn my back on my principles in order to make more money. I often tell people that God owns a whole lot more than anyone else could pay me.

Not long ago, I shared some of the things the Messiah was showing me and doing in my life with a pastor I know, a great guy. He seemed very excited about what I said, so I sent him some of my teaching tapes. I was a little puzzled when he didn't call back, and I kept thinking about him. I followed up and called him again several times.

Finally, about two months after we had first spoken I contacted him and we talked. I asked, "Did you listen to the tapes?"

"Reggie, I'm going to be honest with you. I haven't," he said. "The reason I haven't is because I know if I do and what I hear is true, I'm going to have to preach it. And I know that if I preach it, I'm going to lose some of my people." He admitted that speaking out on certain issues would threaten his lavish lifestyle.

"I appreciate your honesty," I told him. "I'm going to be honest with you. I know that's why you didn't call me. I know right now you're concerned with your lifestyle. I thank God I'm not in your position."

The Bible says, "He who has found his life shall lose it, and he who has lost his life for My sake shall find it" (Mt. 10:39). Martin Luther King Jr. did not "save" his life. He laid it down for what he believed, and this one person changed the destiny of this nation. He achieved true greatness because he refused to compromise. He was a real man.

MEN IN CHRISTIANITY AND ISLAM

The weakness and compromise many exhibit is widespread throughout the church, and it sends the wrong message to the men in particular. One of my cousins was a believer who became so turned off by the image of Christian masculinity that he became a Muslim. I was so surprised that I contacted him and asked him, "What happened?"

He said, "Man, I got sick of the church and the way they handle their business, and the men were weak. In Islam the men seem to present themselves stronger."

My cousin's experience was not uncommon. The black church in America has lost its understanding of the position of its men. Although women have done a good job minding the store, the church will never become fully empowered until men assume their God-ordained leadership role.

Several years ago, a pastor from California surveyed a thousand unchurched black men and asked the question: "Why did you leave a Christian church?" Virtually every man said they left the church because they didn't see any male role models there; women were running the church.

These men agreed that they would become interested in a church that represented a stronger male image. They also felt that Louis Farrakhan and the Nation of Islam projects a healthier male role model than modern Christian church leadership does.

As believers in the Messiah, we obviously don't agree with the doctrines of the Muslim religion. However, the Nation of Islam appeals to black men because it works to restore the image of dignity and strength that our men have been robbed of.

Some churches have done a marvelous job reaching black men. But the church at large has been a dismal failure at reaching out to and restoring the oppressed black man. Neither has it provided black men with accurate historical information concerning slavery and racial injustice.

Consequently, black men are siphoned away from their historical Judeo-Christian roots and converted to the Islamic religion, which teaches that white Christians owned and sold black slaves. It is true that many whites have done dirty deeds in the name of Christianity. But as we'll see, history also reveals that Arabs who practiced the Islamic religion were the chief slave traders.

ISLAM AND ONGOING SLAVERY OF BLACKS

Black historian Dr. Claud Anderson states, "For the purpose of spreading the Islamic religion and taking the mineral wealth of black African nations, the Arabs began enslavement of sub-Saharan blacks in the mid-700s A.D. After nearly 13 centuries, selling an average of one million blacks every hundred years, one can estimate that Arab slave traders enslaved and financially profited from the sale of more than 13 million African blacks."[2]

Even more shocking is the fact that Anderson, in his book entitled *Dirty Little Secrets*, cited evidence that proves that slavery still exists in this day and time. When *The Washington Post* published an article in July 1994 stating that Arabs were still trading black slaves in Mauritania, Ethiopia, and Sudan, various Arab diplomats denied the paper's claim.

When the national press was challenged to prove that slavery still existed in these countries, Anderson said, "*The Baltimore Sun* newspaper accepted the challenge and sent two reporters, one black columnist from *The Sun* and a foreign correspondent, who was white, to Sudan to see if they could buy black slaves and prove beyond a doubt that chattel slavery does exist in Sudan."

"According to *The Washington Post*, the two reporters found clear evidence of slave raids on blacks in the south of Sudan. They actually bought two black slaves from Islamic fundamentalists for the price of $500 each. Having completed their mission, the reporters immediately returned the slaves to their aggrieved families."[3]

Since that report, the slave trading of African Christians by Muslims in northern Africa has become a well-established fact, with scant outrage being voiced by the international community and media. Christian Solidarity International estimates that tens of thousands of children and adults have been snatched from their homes in the southern part of the African nation of Sudan by members of the northern government militia, known as the Popular Defense Force. Some Christian organizations have been set up to purchase these slaves in order to free them, but the practice has not been stopped.

"The government is aiming to completely destroy the social fabric of the Dinka people in this area. They regard them as enemies, because they resist the forced Islamisation and forced Abrabisation policies of the regime," according to a CNN World News report.[4]

The problem is much larger and more pervasive than reported in the media. According to an article posted by the Family Education Network, the number of children being sold into slavery is astonishing. The author, Ricco Villanueva Siasoco, writes:

> The slave trade in Africa was officially banned in the early 1880s, but forced labor continues to be practiced in West and Central Africa today. UNICEF estimates that 200,000 children from this region are sold into slavery each year. Many of these children are from Benin and Togo, and are sold into the domestic, agricultural, and sex industries of wealthier neighboring countries such as Nigeria and Gabon.[5]

Looking to Islam for answers when the world's ongoing slavery arises primarily from Muslim countries is an enormous mistake. This is a perfect example of how history can easily repeat itself if we don't properly understand and avoid the tragic mistakes of the past.

MESSIAH THE MILITANT

We must turn the community of believers back to its purest form. It was not Messiah or the early church fathers who presented male leadership as weak. We must return the blessing of the fathers to the church and restore the strength of uncompromising, masculine leadership.

Attracting men to some churches is a real challenge, because all too often Yeshua has been presented as passive and powerless. But in reality, the Messiah was militant. He confronted the political and religious leaders of His day in a revolutionary fashion, fearlessly challenging their views, and even turning over their tables when they were abusing their positions for greed. Yes, Yeshua was very loving in a powerful way, but He was also radical. He was anything but weak.

We've got to ask God to teach us the way to model true manhood—a manhood based on the Scripture—and we must reject false ideas of manhood. All too often, our definition of manhood depends on the women we sleep with, the kind of cars we drive, or the type of houses we live in. We identify manhood by what we have instead of by what we are—the content of our character.

Grown men and young boys are looking for a solid definition of what it means to be a man. Some of them think that if they deal drugs, they'll be real men. Others feel the need to be involved in a gang; they get involved in gangs because they're looking for a family that accepts them. The gang becomes their substitute for family. Our culture has created a false concept of what community, family, manhood, and womanhood is all about.

The sorry image of masculinity presented by today's church is deeply disturbing to me. Men need leaders who will present the gospel in a way that challenges them to be the type of man God wants them to become, instead of hearing the same tired messages over and over again. As men, we need direction, encouragement, and character-building. Men need leaders who can inspire them to be all that God has called them to be.

We need more relevant messages about the issues we confront on a daily basis. Most preachers today won't even deal with the race issue. People respect Farrakhan's boldness to speak out on issues in a way that could literally get him killed. You might disagree with him, but you have to agree that he's willing to stand up for what he believes.

We can become so concerned about what people think about us that we won't preach the Word of God in an uncompromised way. I respect individuals who boldly proclaim what they believe, regardless of what people think. That's the kind of man I want to be.

Too many people determine who their heroes are based on what those people do and not on how they live. Even in the church, we make heroes of ministers based upon the content of their sermons and not on the content of their character. And we need to research the Word of God to make sure that what they've said is accurate and true. Often, we listen to a sermon expecting to be entertained, not challenged to greater godliness. We've elevated too many preachers to celebrity status; we pack out their meetings and buy their books and support their ministries.

Our greatest heroes, though, should be our parents. The lives of godly parents should inspire us to develop our character and expand our hopes and dreams and plans for the future.

If we trade the virtue of leaders such as Martin Luther King Jr. for celebrities who entertain us and make us laugh, we could be selling our birthright for a mess of pottage, just as Esau did. Sowing to the wind of showmanship and carnal compromise will reap a whirlwind of emptiness and despair. And the legacy we leave our children will be little but chaff driven away by the wind.

MALE BONDS AND GODLY BROTHERHOOD

The leadership in our churches must support and strengthen the leadership of men in our homes. Far too often, church leaders fail to do this. A pastor can provide an excellent source of accountability for husbands. But his interference can also go too far and even undermine a couple's relationship. Whether knowingly or unknowingly, some pastors take away the husband's authority as the head of his household.

Wives also play a role in undermining the husband's authority. All too often, when a man begins to step into his God-ordained position of leadership in the family, his wife continues to depend too much on their pastor. Wives must never neutralize the authority of the husband and father within his home by taking it away from him and giving it to the pastor. Some husbands resent their pastors because they feel they've had their authority undermined; some wives seem to depend more on their pastor than on their husband.

74

When that happens, husbands can begin to feel as if they have to compete for what is already their own, and that is extremely frustrating. Some women are more attracted to their celebrity pastors than they are to their husbands. These pastors, enjoying the admiration of the women, begin to subtly encourage this drawing away of affection. Instead of affirming the spiritual leadership of the men in the congregation, these pastors usurp their role.

As a result, some women lose respect for their husband as a spiritual leader. A pastor or another spiritual leader should never undermine a man's position in the heart of his own wife. Yet, this happens frequently, in subtle and not-so-subtle ways. Small wonder that men become alienated from the church.

In his book *The Principles of Fatherhood*, Myles Munroe deals with this issue in a practical manner. He writes:

> Pastors and church leaders should never usurp the authority of husbands and fathers.... It contradicts the Great Commission for the church to compete with the woman's husband, whom they should want to win to Christ. So, when a woman comes to me as a pastor and says, "Pastor, my husband says I cannot come to the meeting that you called, but you are my pastor. What should I do?" My answer is, "You stay with your husband because I am not your father."

> And I even go so far as writing a note to her husband, apologizing for my program conflicting with his schedule, and requesting that he please forgive me. I send his wife back to him....How might that husband respond? He may well be led to Christ because now he

says, "I finally met a pastor who is not trying to compete with me."

He will desire to know more about the God that his wife serves. Why? Because neither God nor the church tries to take his wife from him, but rather teaches her to love and respect him as her husband and the father of their household."[6]

TEAMWORK IN THE CHURCH

If there's any place where teamwork should be modeled, it's in the church. That's what I miss about football. More than anything, I miss the camaraderie and teamwork, joking in the locker room, and flying together on the plane. I thought that once I left the game that I would find the same sense of team spirit in the church. But I was disappointed with what I ended up finding. I discovered that far too many churches don't really work together as a team.

I'd rather be around athletes whose only concern is winning a game than to be around a group of church people who fight each other at every turn, vie for authority, and undermine and backbite one another.

I played ball with men who didn't even know God, and yet they were committed to watching out for me and for my resources. They would watch my back. How I wish we would begin to understand that concept. We in the community of believers are supposed to be more committed to one another than a family is. We fall far short of that kind of loyalty.

PREACHING A SELFISH PROSPERITY MESSAGE

The community of believers will begin to learn mutual commitment and respect among its members when the leaders start to preach and model these virtues from the pulpit. Unfortunately, much of what is being preached from the pulpit today is a selfish prosperity message that doesn't build unity or promote the spiritual dreams of each individual.

Once I heard a lady say from the pulpit, "You need to visualize your Lexus. Go down there on the lot and visualize it, and believe that God is going to give it to you."

I am not opposed to driving nice vehicles—I drive a nice car myself. But shouldn't we be more concerned about advancing God's kingdom than what kind of car we drive? If we focus on prosperity, our focus is all wrong, and our priorities will reflect that. We should be visualizing how we can impact our communities, teach people to start businesses, and reach out to the poor.

The Bible teaches us that we are responsible for one another. We were never intended to walk alone. We've got to become committed to carving out a path for others to follow. That's why the church must stop preaching a prosperity message that does little for the people of God. That kind of message promotes and engenders individual selfishness.

The Bible says that God loved us so much that He gave His Son. How can we become like the Messiah if we do not learn how to give? The prosperity message preached from many pulpits today teaches a kind of faith that expects God to bless *me*. God blesses us to make us a blessing to others. Commitment to God equals commitment to others. We must teach people how to bless this nation, their families, and their communities. It truly is more blessed, and godly, to give than to receive.

BEYOND THE TITHES AND OFFERINGS

Some of our churches focus on tithes and offerings to the neglect of other aspects of godliness that should be taught.

Giving our tithes and offerings is important, but it's no more important than developing a good work ethic, diligence, unity, community, family, and prayer.

In Luke 11:42, the Messiah told the Pharisees that they should tithe, but He confronted them for neglecting to practice other aspects of God's law as well: "But woe unto you, Pharisees! for ye tithe mint and rue and all manner of herbs, and pass over judgment and the love of God: these ought ye to have done, and not to leave the other undone" (KJV).

RUNNING AFTER THE BLESSING

Instead of running after God, some people in the body of Christ run after His blessings. When an evangelist comes to town, people line up for prayer hoping to get blessed. We've lost sight of what blessings really are. We must move beyond self-centeredness and open our eyes to the world around us. Let's take a look at how the concept of blessing in the Bible developed.

In the Hebrew language, the word, *gaymal*, means camel; it suggests a camel taking a load on its back. When the animal arrives at its destination, it then kneels down so the load can be removed and distributed among the people.

The word "kneel" in the Hebrew is the word *barak*. It's also where we get the word "blessing." So the word "camel" is related to the word "blessing." What the camel represented was taking the load of goods to distribute among those in need. Therefore, the origins of the word "blessing" are connected with the concept of blessing others, not ourselves.

A problem arises when we teach people to pursue blessings, because God says that blessings will run after us when we live obediently. Consumerism is perverting the American church. When we obey, blessings will pursue us, and overtake us.

Conversely, the Bible warns that the same will happen with disobedience and the curse. If we disobey, curses will pursue us, overtake us, and destroy us (see Deut. 28).

This suggests that the consequences of sin can be delayed. Some might suppose that God has forgotten or overlooked rebellion and sin. But the Bible assures the sinner that a curse will follow and catch up with him sooner or later. He might be 70 years old by the time it finally arrives, but it will catch up with him in the end.

We wonder why some people have it so hard, but we never consider that a curse might be following him or her—a curse from previous generations. The Bible says the sins of the fathers will be visited on the children to the third and fourth generations (see Ex. 2:5); curses have pursued parents and caught up with their children. If we don't break the curse through forgiveness and obedience, it will pursue our children and our children's children.

Cloaking greed and selfishness in the guise of blessings will have consequences in the end, and those consequences could be long lasting. The Messiah preached a gospel of forgiveness, holiness, mercy, justice, and generosity. We must never be swept away by a gospel that has strayed from the heart of Yeshua's message.

THE TITLES TRAP

Study the Old Testament prophets and you'll see that it was what they did that identified them as prophets, not some self-imposed title. When Samuel walked through the town everyone knew he was a prophet because God let "none of his words fall to the ground" (see 1 Sam. 3:19 KJV).

None of my teammates ever walked into the locker room and called me "Defensive End." They simply called me Reggie, but they understood my position because of what I did. I knew Brett Favre's position, but I never called him "Quarterback." I called him Brett. I never identified the team players by their titles when I addressed them. I knew them through their actions on the field.

In the church we may call a particular person an evangelist, even though she hasn't won a person to Christ in 40 years. We call another person an apostle, but he sits in the back of the church nodding off until the sermon is over and has never started a church in his life.

Having a gift, a calling, or a position in the community of believers is not our identity. We must find our identity in Yeshua, not in our positions in the church or in the world. Your position is important, but it arises from what you do and not from a title. If you are a leader, your acts of leadership will single you out, not your title.

The community of believers cannot sit idly by waiting for the government to create changes to alleviate poverty, correct injustice, and restore our moral fiber. Believers must become mobilized to do the work. The church and its leaders have let the empty pursuit of titles, wealth, and privilege compromise its true purpose. As believers, we must place greater demands on the current religious system, insisting that our money be used to change the community instead of promoting useless programs or enriching a few leaders. We must stop being so impressed by titles and start demanding greater character from our leaders. We must become willing to say, "I don't want to know who you are; I want to know what you are doing to make a difference!"

A DIFFERENT LOOK AT MALACHI

In the book of Malachi, the Messiah rebukes the leaders. God not only rebukes the ancient leaders during the time the book was written, He also prophetically includes leaders who will live in the last days. Here is what God had to say through the prophet:

> *Behold, I send My messenger, and He shall prepare the way before Me: and the Lord, whom ye seek, shall suddenly come to His temple, even the messenger of the covenant, whom ye delight in: behold, He shall come, saith the Lord of hosts. But who may abide the day of His coming? and who shall stand when He appeareth? for He is like a refiner's fire, and like fullers' soap: And He shall sit as a refiner and purifier of silver: and He shall purify the sons of Levi, and purge them as gold and silver, that they may offer unto the Lord an offering in righteousness. Then shall the offering of Judah and Jerusalem be pleasant unto the Lord, as in the days of old, and as in former years. And I will come near to you to judgment; and I will be a swift witness against the sorcerers, and against the adulterers, and against false swearers, and against those that oppress the hireling in his wages, the widow, and the fatherless, and that turn aside the stranger from his right, and fear not Me, saith the Lord of hosts* (Malachi 3:1-6 KJV).

Throughout the chapter, the Messiah appears to be saying, "I want to bless a nation, but you Levites haven't been purified. You're stealing from My people. You're the only ones who are benefiting from what I've intended for them."

That's what we see today. A lot of preachers have been enriching themselves with the tithes and offerings and the benefits of God instead of using them to bless God's people. The tithes of God's people should be helping the entire community: the Levites, the orphans, the widows, the strangers, and the poor.

RESOURCE ABUSE IN THE CHURCH

Tithes were placed in the storehouse over a period of time ensure that the community had enough resources. The Levites—those whose lives were devoted to ministry—were to consider the Lord to be their inheritance (see Deut. 10:9; 12:12; Num. 18:20-23). God intended for the Levites to be cared for by the people so that they could minister in the temple and teach the people. It was God who took care of the Levites through the people. The Levites didn't have to preach on tithes and offerings. Because the people feared God, they obeyed Him in this matter without needing to be prodded.

The mismanagement of funds by the ancient Levites brought a curse upon them (see Mal. 2:1-2). Too often we exalt our ministers, setting them up on a pedestal that God never intended for them to be placed on. Often they exalt themselves. We treat our ministers as if they were God, and they've come to expect that kind of treatment.

Once I asked a very well known preacher to come and address the football players at our chapel before a game. His people called me back and said he needed a limousine and a full security detail.

I attempted to explain that I merely wanted him to come and speak to our players, not to an enormous crowd of people. It was not our policy to pay people to come and speak in a chapel service. His demands bothered me, because I respected him.

I decided that if he didn't want to come and speak, that was fine. But I was getting ready to play a football game, and I didn't have the time to put together a security team and hire a limousine. (I never had my own personal limousine or security when I played, and some of those fans can really be rough!) The preacher declined the invitation. I was trying to give him a chance to speak into the lives of some very influential athletes, and he missed out on that opportunity.

THE ROLE OF TODAY'S CHURCH

I'm deeply disturbed by the tainted spiritual climate in the church today. Consumerism and self-indulgence often have replaced the commitment we once felt to righteous living, community, charity, and obedience to God. Martin Luther King Jr. once said, "If the church does not recapture its prophetic zeal, it will become an irrelevant social club without moral or spiritual authority." That's happened to many of today's religious establishments.

It's important for believers to be obedient in tithes and offerings. But I hope that if I'm ever obedient *only* in the area of tithes and offerings, God would cause me to lose everything I have. Why? It would mean that I had lost my way. If I'm not obedient to God in every area of my life, then all my tithes and offerings will count as nothing when I stand before Him.

CHURCH LEADERS

Too often politicians and preachers want to hold on to power by keeping people in ignorance, because ignorance is a powerful tool. It's a tactic that has been used throughout history. The only way to break the power of ignorance is to expose people to the truth.

We've got far too many politicians and motivational speakers in the pulpit. We need the Word of God to be spoken from the pulpit without compromise and without questionable motives and agendas.

Many of today's spiritual leaders are taking the Word of God and attempting to fit it in to their personal version of the "truth." God's absolute truth should never be changed or compromised to fit in to the popular thinking of any man, culture, or time period.

When we finally hear unadulterated truth being spoken with boldness and love from the pulpits across America, this nation's people, both black and white, will be inspired to rise up and claim our greatest promise—our true spiritual destiny.

ENDNOTES

1. Jim Haskins, *I Have a Dream* (Brookfield, CT: The Millbrook Press, 19921), pp. 95-96.

2. Claud Anderson, *Dirty Little Secrets* (Bethesda, MD: PowerNomics Corporation of America Publishers, 1997), p. 49.

3. Ibid.

4. "Buying the freedom of slaves in the Sudan," CNN Interactive; 20 December 1997: www.cnn.com/WORLD/9712/20/sudan.slavery.

5. Ricco Villanueva Siasoco, "Modern Slavery," Family Education Network; 18 April 2001: www.factmonster.com/spot/slavery1.html.

6. Myles Munroe, *The Principles of Fatherhood* (Lanham, MD: Pneuma Life Publishers, 2001) n.p.

CHAPTER FIVE

MANHOOD: THE FATHER'S BLESSING

Fatherhood

We must combine the toughness of a serpent and the softness of a dove, a tough mind and a tender heart.
—**Martin Luther King Jr.**

SEVERAL YEARS AGO, my kids got into the Pokémon craze. They spent tons of money collecting giant stacks of Pokémon cards. The product line offered a plethora of comic books, videos, toys, DVDs, television cartoons, video games, and a wildly popular collectible card game. The whole thing seemed innocent enough, but something about the whole craze bothered me. Every time I looked at the cards I was confronted with this nagging at my spirit that I couldn't quite identify. I just didn't feel good about Pokémon.

At one point, another father seemed to confirm this nagging concern I had about these cards. He said one of his children had started getting migraine headaches, but they stopped after he made him get rid of the cards. He felt the youngster's headaches were somehow linked to the cards.

What I didn't realize at the time was the company producing these cards was also responsible for creating Dungeons & Dragons, a game known for drawing children deep into the occult.

As a Christian father committed to building a godly home, I was aware that the Bible warns against owning occult paraphernalia and becoming involved in occult activities, such as Ouija boards, tarot cards, fortune-telling, and séances. Deuteronomy 18:10-12 affirms the fact that dark powers can be linked to such activities—powers that bring curses into the lives of their unwitting victims.

At this point all I had was a nagging sense that something about these cards was not right. I drove home thinking about this child's migraines and the words of a father that so strongly confirmed my gut feelings about the nature of this game. I made up my mind to deal with the issue.

Once I got home, I gathered my family around me and began explaining my feelings about Pokémon. However, what started as a concerned father's effort to oversee the spiritual development of his kids quickly turned into a challenge to my leadership position in the family as father.

I sat my children down, took a seat next to my wife, and tried to explain how I felt. "Look, I'm convinced that something is not right about this Pokémon game, and I want you to throw away all of your Pokémon stuff," I said.

My two children challenged me, and my wife joined in by taking their side. This was particularly upsetting to me, because Sara has long supported me in the decisions I've made as husband and father.

"Well, Dad, you do things that aren't really right. You watch wrestling."

Now my children were challenging me. This difficult situation was compounded by my wife's open disagreement. I wanted her to stand with me in front of the children and voice any disagreements later in private, but her challenges became increasingly intense.

I was having a difficult time explaining why I felt so strongly about the matter. I just had a strong, intuitive sense deep down that the game had the power to harm my children.

Sara insisted, "If you're opposed to the Pokémon stuff, then you need to tell me why!"

We argued back and forth for a while, and eventually I just told them to forget it. I walked upstairs and went to bed, but I couldn't sleep at all that night.

As the sun was rising, I got everybody up. "Come downstairs. We need to talk," I said.

I sat all three of them down and said, "Look guys, sometimes when God speaks into the heart of a father He doesn't give him all the details. This can make it difficult to always give a complete explanation for why he feels a particular way. Nevertheless, I do know that God is impressing in my heart that all of this stuff should be thrown away. So that's the way it's going to be."

My son was very upset, but I stood my ground. "That's the way it's going to be. You all go upstairs. You're going to get all your cards, and you're going to throw them away," I said.

I turned to Sara and said, "You disagreed with me in front of our children, and that shouldn't happen."

At this point, Pokémon was not the issue. The underlying issue was my leadership responsibility for my family. That position had been challenged, and I needed to take it back. There is a blessing of protection, provision, and instruction that's been invested in me as head of my family, and I cannot impart the blessing if I forfeit my place and position.

A few years later, the kids told me that they were glad I had taken this stand. I know it provided them with a deep sense of security and peace to see me as their protector, even in matters they couldn't fully understand.

THE FATHER'S BLESSING

As fathers, our position is powerful, as is our responsibility. We've been entrusted with an ability to make a dramatic difference in the future of our children and our children's children. The blessings of the father that we impart will live on for many generations.

The story of two biblical patriarchs, Jacob and Isaac, illustrate the power of the father's blessing. Genesis 27 outlines the story of Jacob receiving his father's blessing deceitfully, a blessing that, notwithstanding the deceit, positioned him as the inheritor and next patriarch of Israel.

Why was Jacob so desperate to get a blessing from Isaac that he was willing to deceive him to get it? He understood the power of the father's blessing. He knew that when his father blessed him, it would make a great difference in his life. Throughout the Old Testament, it's evident that some of the children were desperate to get a blessing from their fathers. Jacob—the one who stole his brother's blessing—eventually would pass on the father's blessing to all of his sons, the 12 patriarchal tribe leaders of the nation of Israel.

MISSING THE BLESSING—THE HARD FACTS

Today's fathers don't bless their children as they should. They don't give them their approval. Children often look to their mothers for love, and they usually receive it. But they need the approval of their fathers—they need the fathers' blessing. Without the blessing, our children are launched into adulthood with a deep sense of need. That's one of the reasons why our society is in so much trouble today.

Statistics bear this out. During the days of slavery, a black child was more likely to grow up living with both parents than he or she is today.[1] As recently as 1960, three-quarters of Africa-Americans were born into a family of a married couple.[2] Today, only one-third of black children have two parents in the home.[3]

"Black children are only half as likely as white children to be living in a two-parent household, and are eight times more likely than white children to live with an unwed mother. For black children under six, the most common arrangement—applying to 42 percent of them—was to live with a never-married mother," according to author Maggie Gallagher.[4]

Across the board, poverty rates are highest where the father is absent. And in the black community, the challenges continue to be the greatest. Only 30 percent of black babies are born to two-parent families, while in other ethnic categories the figure is about 75 percent. More than 40 percent of black babies are born to mother-only households, in contrast to less than 20 percent in other ethnic categories.[5]

Although white children were the largest single ethnic group of young children in poverty, the overall population percentages are much higher for blacks. In 1994, 2.2 million young white children were living in poverty compared to 1.9 million young black children and 1.7 million young Hispanic children.[6]

Poverty, it seems, is very closely linked to lack of the father's blessing—and his absence from the household.

RECLAIMING THE BLESSING

Robbed of the father's blessing, American children, and especially black American children, are abandoned, left to endure poverty, high crime rates, low educational levels, early disease, and despair. I contend that in order to reclaim our children, our dignity, and our wealth, we must reclaim the father's blessing. Without it, the decline will continue, and our children's future and hope will be wasted in disappointment and hopelessness. Fathers must be restored to their rightful place.

One of the things I love about Orthodox Jewish communities is the way they have cherished and guarded the father's blessing and the role of father within their closely-knit communities. Orthodox Jews diligently teach their children: Men mentor the boys, and women mentor the girls. They understand that for a boy to know what it is to be a man, he needs to see how men act and what men do. It's the same with respect to girls and women. At the age of 13, young men celebrate their bar mitzvah, a ceremony in which the community announces and honors a boy's transition to manhood. A similar ceremony, a bat mitzvah, is held to celebrate a girl's transition to womanhood.

In contemporary American pop culture, particularly on television commercials and sitcoms, fathers are often portrayed as bumbling, inept, clueless, and less than intelligent. Kids are usually the smart ones in the families, followed by their wise-cracking mothers. The fathers never seem to "get it." Those male stereotypes work against the valuable masculine role within our families, communities, and society.

The world's three most prominent religions—Christianity, Judaism, and Islam—place a great emphasis on the role of the father in rearing healthy families. As the importance of religion has declined in American culture, so has the emphasis placed on fatherhood.

THE IMPORTANCE OF COVENANT

Our culture suffers because fathers and leaders no longer understand the importance of an extremely significant biblical concept—the concept of covenant. In ancient times, covenants were vitally important. If a man broke a covenant with his family, he would be hunted down and killed. Honorable men would actually die for other people in order to keep a covenant vow.

A powerful picture of biblical covenant is illustrated in Genesis 16 when God and Abraham entered into covenant together. Abraham cut an animal in half and spread the pieces on the ground; and God walked through the center of the two halves. God's presence was indicated by a flame that was seen moving through the path between the carcass pieces. In ancient terms, the ritual expressed each party's willingness to die for the other person. It also suggested that death would occur if either party were to break the covenant.

Our lack of understanding of the importance of covenants in modern times has caused us to lose the sense of loyalty that the ancients felt towards their families. God commanded the fathers in Israel to teach their children (see Deut. 4:9); teaching was to be one of the most important aspects of their existence. Since then, descendants of the ancient Hebrews have maintained a mindset of investing their resources—money, time, and energy—in their children, educating them in the covenants of God.

Once we break covenant with God, it becomes all too easy for us to break covenant with our families. When Isaac met Rebekah he brought her into his tent and married her by consummating their vows. He had not yet seen her, for she had a veil covering her face. The Bible indicates that he fell in love with her after they were married, not before. Isaac's love for Rebekah was a "learned" love.

What we consider falling in love today is often little more than lust. Men become infatuated with women without realizing the responsibility that comes with genuine love, marriage, and fatherhood; the children that result from their relationship will need a father who is committed to them.

The single most important thing a man can do when he begins to build a family is to bring his children up in the ways of God. Being a pastor begins in the home, for all men must become a pastor to their households by providing an example of loyalty and respect to God, wives, and children.

The Jewish community's commitment to mentoring its sons and daughters is the basis for the apostle Paul's admonition that older women teach the younger women and that older men teach younger ones (see Tit. 2:3-6). The mentoring role of one generation toward another held an important place in the education of young people.

Unfortunately, many people are unaware of the importance of that tradition. Their own parents did not lead *them* by example, and as a result they've failed to become adults who lead *their* children by example. American children tend to spend the majority of their time with other children, and they continue to act like kids long into their 20s and 30s. The truth is, they're modeling all that they've ever known. They enter into adulthood ill-equipped, seldom having been around real men and real women who could teach them what adulthood, leadership, responsibility, citizenship, and parenting is all about.

UNWED MOTHERS

Another critical problem in our communities is that far too many kids are being born out of wedlock; the fathers are not in the home, and the mothers are forced into unnatural parenting situations. The best mother in the world still does not know what it is to be a man, and she cannot adequately impart the father's blessing to a son or daughter. Adding to this curse is the unfortunate fact that many of these mothers have not even been trained to be women.

One of the results is an abundance of young boys who are out of control, who have never had an opportunity to sit down and talk to a man or spend time with a man to really see how a man acts. Teachers, mothers, social workers, judges, and preachers point their fingers into the faces of these youngsters and tell them to act like men. But they don't know how to be men, because they haven't really been around men.

We can't simply preach at these boys and expect significant results. We've got to show them what manhood is by our words, actions, and example. This mentoring role is one more aspect of the father's blessing; it means that godly men in the community of believers must not restrict their role as fathers to their own households. We must become fathers in our communities by becoming mentors to fatherless boys.

This lack of the father's blessing, this inability to understand and learn manhood through the mentoring of elders, has created a generation of immature men in the community of believers, and in government. We've released generations of leaders into positions that they're not equipped to handle.

THE HEARTS OF THE FATHERS

Where are the true role models for today's young people? We are quick to criticize their lifestyles but slow to get involved in their lives. Although community-sponsored programs such as Big Brothers and Big Sisters of America are helping, those efforts are of minuscule impact in proportion to the vastness of the problem. The programs work well, but so much more must be done in order to turn the situation around.

Malachi 4:5-6 teaches: "Behold, I will send you Elijah the prophet...And he shall turn the heart of the fathers to the children, and the heart of the children to their fathers..." (KJV). I believe this Scripture has a three-pronged interpretation. He will restore fathers to families; he will restore fathers to communities: and he will restore the place of honor and respect for our ancestral fathers as well—including the fathers of our faith, such as Abraham, Isaac, and Jacob (which, among other interpretations, means he will restore the breech between Jewish and Christian believers in Jehovah). God promises to move in the earth to restore the hearts of the children to the fathers, and the hearts of the fathers to the children. God Himself will restore the father's blessing.

MANHOOD AND COMMUNITY

True manhood finds its definition within the context of Judeo-Christian thought. Therefore, we must begin to understand manhood as it is established in the Bible. If we don't understand manhood as taught by our biblical forefathers, we'll end up teaching a false manhood. The kind of manhood our spiritual forefathers established produced some of the greatest men who ever walked on the face of the earth.

Abraham, the great father of our faith, was invested in building a community. His commitment to community gave definition to his manhood. We would be wise to begin to understand biblical manhood as it is placed within community. Attempting to identify manhood outside of community will lead to a false manhood, a manhood founded on independence and personal isolation rather than true masculine expression. Abraham, Isaac, Jacob, Moses, David, Joseph, and other biblical examples expressed their manhood through a patriarchal position of leadership—a masculinity that empowered their community. By their example, we see that biblical manhood is positional and relational, and that position is located and expressed within community.

Much of the power of Judeo-Christian manhood has been diluted and diminished in our current experience.

ROLE MODELS AND HEROES

Martin Luther King Jr. said, "I have a dream that my four little children will one day live in a nation where they will not be judged by the color of their skin, but by the content of their character." King was a hero who understood that the cost of being a hero required more than having your face on television. To King, being a hero meant paying the price through your character and integrity.

Instead of making men of faith, integrity, and character our heroes, we've made heroes out of actors and athletes solely because of what they've accomplished in their professions. When did we stop looking to people of strong character and moral integrity to be our heroes? Today, some people are considered heroes even though they've been arrested, used drugs, or done other illegal or immoral things.

King was a radical revolutionary who fought for truth and justice with the righteousness of God's Word. He stood up against unparalleled challenges as a devout, relentless Christian soldier who died for what he believed in. Even his methods of nonviolent resistance were radical and courageous, despite the attempts of other militant groups to reject such tactics as ineffectual and worthless. King did more for black people in America than any other leader of the twentieth century did. He was a father to the black community, and we benefited greatly from the father's blessing he bestowed.

Where do we learn what true leadership is? And how do we pass those values on to subsequent generations? Once again, it is the father's blessing that teaches our sons and daughters who to count as heroes. When the father is absent or his presence is rare, then young people are forced to find their heroes elsewhere, most often through the media. When a father takes his place in the family and in his community, his sons and daughters learn whom to admire and respect and model their own lives after. Imparting values, instilling truth, and inspiring dreams are a father's job. How can those who were never taught to be a father learn how to succeed in this vital role?

DRUG DEALERS AND BUSINESSMEN

We need positive role models like legitimate black entrepreneurs and successful businesspeople instead of drug dealers and prostitutes. When our children are surrounded every day by leaders of despair, they end up believing there is no hope for them. They need to be able to look around and see a broad spectrum of possibilities modeled through the lives of business leaders, entrepreneurs, doctors, lawyers, tradesmen, and teachers. Unfortunately, the only business role models some of these kids see every day are the drug dealers, pimps, and prostitutes, because that's the big business their communities offer.

Many young black males feel that the only way they can make it in life is by playing a professional sport. Such an unrealistic expectation only sets these kids up for failure. But other young people are smart enough to realize right away that the odds are stacked against them; they know they must find ways to survive. Some of these kids could probably be better businessmen than many people who run large corporations. Unfortunately, they turn to illegal and immoral ways of making money because they have no hope. They don't realize that through Christ all things are possible, even in the midst of poverty and prejudice. They've degraded their entrepreneurial skills into drug trafficking and other forms of crime.

I've been fortunate to work in a profession that gave me a chance. But that wasn't always the case; as recently as the late 1960s, some of the most gifted black athletes in the world couldn't get a break. Back then, there were those who wouldn't dare let a black player compete on their teams. All that changed when teams with black players began trouncing them.

In professional baseball, it wasn't until April 15, 1947, that Jackie Robinson, the 28-year-old grandson of a slave, became the first black player to cross over into the major leagues. Robinson's strength and courage as a groundbreaker and harbinger of change was astonishing. At a time when at least 70 percent of southern blacks lived in deep poverty and endured the indignities of segregated schools, churches, parks, beaches, buses, trains, hotels, restrooms, and drinking fountains, Jackie broke through. It was also a time when black Americans continued to be lynched in the South.

A native of Mississippi, Robinson had been intolerant of racial abuse from childhood. Branch Rickey, owner and manager of the Brooklyn Dodgers, was aware of the further abuse Robinson would face, so he tested and taunted him before signing him on. The Boston Globe writes:

> For hours, Rickey, a devout man who forbade profanity, posed as a hotel manager, an outraged headwaiter, a ballplayer from the South, and a Southern sportswriter,

hurling every insult imaginable in the face of the proud Robinson, taunting and testing him.

"Mr. Rickey," an anguished Robinson finally cried out, "do you want a ballplayer who's afraid to fight back?"

"I want a ballplayer with guts enough not to fight back," Rickey replied. "You will symbolize a crucial cause. One incident, just one incident, can set it back 20 years."[7]

Robinson walked courageously through a wall of racial hatred to open the gates wide enough for other players to enter through. At his funeral, it was said of him: "This man turned the stumbling block into a stepping stone."[8]

It was the exceptional ability of black athletes, as well as their character, that led to the integration of professional sports. Had these men not displayed amazing talent and irreproachable character, that integration might never have happened. When men like Jim Brown came into the NFL—Brown was signed by the Cleveland Browns in 1957—and began to dominate the game, owners and investors started realizing that not allowing black athletes to play was a bad business decision. Though many managers and owners continued to be deeply prejudiced, they were also interested in winning. Eventually, they came to respect black athletes for their abilities and for the character and professionalism they displayed.

ROLE MODELS AND MENTORS

Years ago, men like Robinson would return to black communities to set up sports camps and impart something to the next generation. Today, many of the football camps are located in suburban areas. They're close to the cities, but still a little too far for inner-city kids to attend. That's why when I set up a camp for kids, I try to locate it right in the heart of the inner city to reach as many needy youngsters as possible.

The policies of integration spawned an exodus of upper- and middle-class blacks away from the communities that need their influence. These successful, well-educated leaders might have provided positive role models for less fortunate young people had they stayed. As some of us advanced, many were left behind—especially the children.

Many of these kids can't find positive role models who are successful in their communities. Some leaders oversimplify the problem and tell them to pull themselves up by the bootstraps. But many of them don't have any bootstraps to pull up; they need a helping hand.

The simple truth is that although a great deal of opportunity exists in the world, some people don't have the same opportunities as others. Those of us who have been more fortunate must reach out to help level the playing field. If I pull myself up without trying to pull my brother up with me, then my success isn't really worth much.

True success involves helping the less fortunate, and this help must come primarily through the church and the community. There are a lot of athletes who have attempted to help, but placing a problem of this magnitude at the feet of a few ballplayers is not only an unrealistic responsibility but also an unfair expectation.

Change is going to have to come through community-minded people who want to make sure that their children are taught their values. Our communities must stop allowing people to come into our children's lives whose values are completely different from our own. We cannot let those who oppose our values inject their beliefs into our children.

Interestingly, in Hasidic communities where parents are devoted to imparting their values to their children, there is little or no crime. A little leaven leavens the whole lump, according to the Word of God; we need to fight those negative outside influences that conspire to corrupt our children's morals. We cannot expect our children to have good morals if we fail to pull them away from immoral influences.

Many athletes are trying to help the underprivileged. Individuals like NFL running back Warrick Dunn have been known to make down payments on homes for low-income single mothers. Others, like former Super Bowl champion Keith Jackson, sponsor tutorial programs. Jackson realized enormous success in the lives of youngsters who once were flunking out of school. Following his program, many of them ended up getting scholarships to attend college.

There are a lot of dedicated guys who are doing some great things in their communities, and most of them will never get any recognition for it. These men are doing their part to fill the void and impart the father's blessing. They are filling the role of father figure to a generation of lost, often fatherless young boys and girls. If their efforts could be combined with the efforts of others and united with resources beyond their own private funds, the impact of what they're trying to accomplish could be so much greater.

MENTORING A LOST GENERATION

The relationship with a father figure—an individual who is a mentor—should always be like a relationship between a real son and his father. When my son wants to talk to me, he feels comfortable to just come on in to wherever I happen to be, sit down, and share his thoughts and his heart with me because he trusts me.

My son also understands and respects my position. I love him, and he loves me. I'm going to give him advice. I'm going to correct him when he needs to be corrected, I'm going to be firm when discipline is required, and I'm going to admit I'm wrong whenever I'm wrong.

That's how the father figure should be viewed, even in the mentoring position of leadership within the community at large. Community fathers should be relatable, accessible, caring, and willing to give. Although the strength of a protector and provider should be most prominent in the home, the community can contribute by understanding and taking refuge in the community fathers worthy of their trust.

The father's role in a relationship is based on an understanding and respect for the father's position of authority. A son enjoys that relationship, desiring to draw from the father wisdom, knowledge, provision, and protection. He wants his father to teach him and correct him when he's wrong.

As fathers in our community, we need to make sure that our sons and daughters are being reared in the community. That means living before them as a godly leader within the community. What we place within our sons and daughters by way of example will stay with them. The Bible tells parents to "train up a child in the way he should go, and when he is old he will not depart from it" (Prov. 22:6 KJV).

Business people must be willing to impart wisdom and business acumen to the young. Young leaders need to be able to count on the support of experienced preachers and business people. Too often when a potential leader is trying to find his way, he experiences an attitude that tells him, "You've got to go through the process I've gone through. You've got to learn it all again starting from square one."

I've heard fathers say to their sons, "If you work as hard as I do you can be as successful as I am." Expressed in that way, it sounds almost as if the father would prefer that his son not succeed. A better way to encourage the son would be to say, "Son, I'm going to teach you everything I know so that you can be more successful than I am."

Jerome Edmonson is providing a community mentoring role through his organization, the Christian Business Network. Our urban organization, Urban Hope, is also meeting this need through training, mentoring, and networking to help young businessmen and women develop business plans and skill and find funds to get started.

Being a community father implies a willingness to impart the treasure of experience, wisdom, insight, and knowledge to the generations coming up behind us. The sons in our communities need us to impart the mantle to them. They need to learn how to avoid pitfalls. They should never feel sting of rejection that says, "You've got to go through all the bumps and the bruises, and you need to learn the hard way because that's what I went through."

Don't force a young man to start from the same place you had to start from and go through the entire process of discovery all over again. Show him how to avoid the mistakes you made and be proud of him when he advances beyond you. His success is a reflection on you, when you've taken your place of leadership within your community.

I often tell my kids that I don't want them to do some of the things I did. I don't want my son or my daughter to learn that it's a mistake to have sex before marriage by actually having sex before marriage.

My son Jeremy has always been an honest kid. When he was eight years old, Jeremy was calling me almost every day at training camp because he was dealing with issues related to women and sex. He had opened up a magazine and saw women in bikinis, and I guess he felt guilty for looking at those types of pictures. He actually called me to confess, saying, "Dad, I opened up the magazine and I saw this woman with a bikini on, and another woman had nothing but her bra on. I'm sorry."

I took a few minutes and tried to explain that he hadn't done anything wrong. But he continued calling me every day. "Dad, I turned the TV on and this woman didn't have any clothes on," he would say, or something like that.

I realized he was starting to deal with his own sexuality, but he was also wearing me out. My wife, Sara, started calling on his behalf. He would get on the phone and start confessing every thought.

Frustrated while driving home one day, I prayed, "God, I've got to tell him to stop. This is simple stuff." The Lord spoke very clearly to my heart. "Why?"

I said, "Because he is wearing me out." God spoke again, "Don't you do that. You be honest with him."

I decided that it was time for my wife and me to sit the children down and talk to them about sex. My son was eight and my daughter was six, but we told them everything. I had come to the conclusion that they needed to hear the facts from us, not from some outside source. It was important for them to understand how special sex can be within the context of marriage, and how painful and destructive it can be outside of marriage.

When Jeremy started asking questions, the first thing that hit me was the fact that he had beat me at video games when he was only three years old. If he was intelligent enough to beat me in those video games and to understand how to operate a computer, his mind was also intelligent enough to hear about sex. I wanted to instill in him a sense of morality regarding sexual choices. And I also wanted to emphasize how beautiful sex could be one day when he is married.

FATHER KNOWS BEST

A friend of mine shared a story with me about his daughter's marriage that underscored the respect a man can receive when he's willing to lay hold of his position as father in an uncompromising way. Ralph, a Jewish rabbi who is a believer, had a pretty daughter whom a young man wanted to date. While driving on a road trip, Ralph listened to a popular radio psychologist talk about how a lot of youth pastors were caught up in sex scandals with young girls in their churches. When Ralph heard that, he decided to discourage the relationship between the young man, who was a youth pastor, and his daughter.

Ralph's daughter was crazy about the young man and butted heads with him over the matter. Ralph decided that he would meet with him—and make him sign a contract. Basically, he created a contract that was so strict he was sure it would cause the young man to back off from his daughter. These were some of the terms: The boy would have to sit under his teaching for a year. He would have to take six months of Hebrew language courses. He would not be permitted to speak to his daughter for an entire year. If he ran in to her in public, he could say hello and no more. He could have absolutely no other contact with her.

Amazingly, he signed the contract, took Ralph's course, and was deeply moved by Ralph's teachings. Three years later this young man and Ralph's daughter were married. Both were virgins, the young man never made a move toward her throughout their courtship. He respected all that Ralph had asked him to do. The way Ralph had taught his daughter and the process that he had taken this young man through had left a great impact on them. They were both deeply challenged to seek a closer relationship with God. The wedding was all the more beautiful because of their sexual purity and because they had worked so hard to prove themselves in order to earn the father's blessing.

Although I'm not suggesting we separate our kids and make them write contracts, this kind of arrangement echoes something we've lost. Historically, the position of father over a home and father within a community elicited great respect and genuine honor. In previous centuries, Ralph's story would not have been unusual. What was so interesting to me was that although Ralph's rules were designed to be somewhat harsh, when the young people accepted them, they were genuinely blessed. A father is entrusted by God with enormous power to bless.

HONOR YOUR FATHER

I recall the day a five-year old boy walked up to me and said, "Here, sign this." I'm thinking, *Where did he get this disrespectful attitude?* So I said, "No, I'm not signing that."

"Oh yeah, you sign this," he demanded. Then he started putting it in my hand, and he said, "You sign this now!" I bent down and asked, "How old are you?"

"I'm five," he spat out the words with defiance. I said, "Well, I'm 40, and when you come back and ask me right, then I'll give you my autograph."

The little guy got louder and more insistent, "No, you're going to sign it!"

I walked away from him.

His mother got hold of him. We were doing a grand opening for his mother's business, and she was very embarrassed. She grabbed him and said, "You go over and you apologize."

Now, sheepishly, he said, "I'm sorry. Could you sign this?" I asked him, "Well, what's the magic word?"

And he said, "Please." "Sure," I said. "What's my name?"

He respectfully answered, "Mr. White. Could you please sign this, Mr. White?"

I finally gave him my autograph.

One of the negative features of professional sports is that people disrespect you, even the kids. They get so used to seeing you as Reggie on TV that they think it's appropriate to say, "Hey, Reggie." But I tell kids to call me Mr. White. I was brought up to call adults Mr. and Mrs. So if kids want something from me, then I make them address me properly.

The children of Israel were taught to rise in the presence of the elders as a sign of respect. Today, many kids have no respect for older people at all. I believe that the disrespect of elders is partly due to the dissolution of our neighborhoods. If you lived in our community when I was brought up, you were expected to call your elders Mr. or Mrs. Such respect was understood within the confines of the community. However, with the loss of the concept of community came the loss of that kind of respect.

RECLAIMING THE FATHER'S BLESSING

In the biblical story of Jacob and Esau, the elder son Esau held the right to the father's blessing but sold it for a bowl of soup when he was hungry. He foolishly lost the blessing because he didn't value it enough. We must never fall into the same trap. We must respect and honor the father's position to protect, instruct, correct, and bless his family and his community.

As fathers to our communities, we must become mentors to sons and daughters beyond our own. We must never project a sense of superiority, but rather we must allow those whom we mentor to feel they are our equals who have knowledge and direction to impart. A genuine mentor is a friend in the truest sense.

Through football, I learned that true leadership begins when you start to value the man standing next to you. You might not even like him, but you value his place and position. You respect his right to stand there. Eventually, you realize that one of the reasons he's there is to help your to reach your goal. Together you will achieve far more than you ever could alone.

POWER TO BLESS

If God truly is turning the hearts of the sons to the fathers and the fathers to the sons in our time, then reclaiming the honor and respect of our position as fathers will play a vital part in that heart change. The commandment to honor fathers and mothers was the first commandment that came with a promise attached; those who honored their parents could expect to live long lives. Exodus 20:12 says, "Honor you father and your mother, that you days may be prolonged in the land which the Lord your God gives you" (NASB).

Some of that honor and respect to which fathers are entitled must come to us simply by virtue of the power of our expectation. We must assume and command the dignity and respect of our stewardship as fathers as a heavenly grace bestowed upon our position. And we must always walk in our position, not as an entitlement to selfishness but as a grace through which we may bless others.

ENDNOTES

1. Andrew J. Cherlin, *Marriage, Divorce, Remarriage* (Cambridge, MA: Harvard University Press, 1992), p. 110.

2. Christopher Jencks, "Is the American Underclass Growing?" Cited in Maggie Gallagher, *The Abolition of Marriage* (Regnery Publishing; Washington D.C., 1996), p. 117.

3. Dennis A. Ahlburg and Carol J. DeVita, "New Realities of the American Family," *Population Bulletin 47*; August 1992, p. 8.

4. Maggie Gallagher, *The Abolition of Marriage*; p. 117, citing Andrew J. Cherlin, *Marriage, Divorce, Remarriage* (Cambridge, MA: Harvard University Press, 1992), pp. 98-99.

5. The Census Bureau and www.thuban.com/census/index.html.

6. www.cpmcnet.Columbia.edu/dept/nccp/reports/longterm.html.

7. Gordon Edes, "Opening a New, Wide World: Robinson's Impact Felt Well Beyond Chalk Lines," *The Boston Globe*; 28 March 1997: www.boston.com/globe/specialreports/1997/mar/robinson.

8. Ibid.

SOLUTIONS AND ANSWERS: MOVING TO THE NEXT LEVEL

CHAPTER SIX

ECONOMICS AND THE BLACK AMERICAN COMMUNITY

Even when a Negro manages to grasp a foothold
on the economic ladder, discrimination remains to push
him off after he has ascended a few rungs. It hounds him
at every level, to stultify his initiative and insult his being.
For the pitiful few who climb into economic security
it persists and closes different doors to them.
—Martin Luther King Jr.

W E NEED TO SEE MORE PEOPLE in the black community gain access to the basic opportunities necessary to rise above the poverty level. When I was growing up, I was content because my grandmother, mother, and stepfather worked very hard to provide the basic necessities of life. We never really considered ourselves poor, because we lived within our means.

Far too many black kids are growing up in unacceptable living conditions. Housing projects are substandard. I grew up in projects with my grandmother, so I'm well aware of the poverty that exists in them. Near the projects and my high school were creeks that often flooded, turning yards into a great lake. The field where we played ball as youngsters was nothing more than an open garbage dump.

Today's housing projects and inner-city schools are rat infested, run down, and lacking in the basic necessities that are taken for granted in more affluent communities. Many black children are forced to grow up amid an unacceptable degree of lack. As we've seen earlier, poverty levels among black youngsters stubbornly remain at high levels. The desperate cry from our communities must be heard and addressed. We must do much better than we are doing.

Unfortunately, much of the funding allocated to these needs has only served to enrich the leaders put in place to address the need. The cry has gone unanswered, and the needs have not been met. Poverty rates have continued to rise. Something must be done. It's time for a change. I would like to turn now and take a close look at economics in the black community, the obstacles, the ongoing need, the great strides and advances, and the possibility of fresh empowerment.

Let's start by taking a look at some of the obstacles that must be overcome if we are to realize the kind of success and change in our communities that we all know is possible. Removing these roadblocks will unleash the forward motion of change that many of us have worked toward for years.

One of the first roadblocks that continues to sabotage our efforts in black American communities is a practice called "redlining."

BLOCKING SUCCESS THROUGH REDLINING

Historically, economic redlining of neighborhoods began when bankers, lending agencies, and insurance companies pulled out maps and circled black neighborhoods with bold red lines. Those living within the redlined area were then deemed outside of the lender's consideration for receiving available funds for purchasing homes, starting businesses, making home improvements, sending kids to college, or purchasing vehicles. The practice was totally race-based, and it continues today, although in more subtle ways.

Throughout the second half of the twentieth century redlining, more than any other practice, has worked behind the scenes to keep black neighborhoods impoverished. A steady influx of government funds to offset the impact of redlining has for the most part been siphoned off by the leadership empowered to disburse those funds. This is one of the major reasons that poverty levels, along with the high crime, poor health, and other characteristics that accompany these levels, remain so high.

In order to see dramatic economic change in our communities, we must seek ways to transcend the hurdles placed in black neighborhoods through ongoing redlining. Our people pay taxes, but they don't receive the services and benefits those taxes were supposed to provide. Our people place their savings in the banks, but the banks are not lending them money.

Let's look at several examples of how redlining has affected blacks.

THE HOME OWNERS LOAN CORPORATION

The origins of the term "redlining" can be traced to the Home Owners Loan Corporation (HOLC) in Dade County, Florida, a federal New Deal agency from the 1930s. This government-sponsored organization created an elaborate appraisal and rating system for different neighborhoods in cities across America. The neighborhoods were plotted on "residential security maps."

The maps were used for many years afterwards as a tool to deny loans to residents of black communities.[1]

A key factor to keep in mind is that these were government New Deal funds that were being poured into communities during the Great Depression in order to restore economic viability to American neighborhoods. Redlining had the effect of excluding black communities from this process.

On these maps, type "A" neighborhoods, circled in blue, were considered the most affluent areas and the most desirable for lending purposes. Type "B," denoted in yellow, were considered slightly less desirable but also good. "C" neighborhoods, circled in green, were generally sparsely populated fringe areas that typically bordered black neighborhoods.

All of the black and low-income neighborhoods were characterized as type "D" and were considered, primarily on the basis of race, to be the worst for lending. Type "D" neighborhoods were circled in red—hence the term "redlining."

You will recall that many black American communities in the first half of the century included affluent, educated, and successful blacks, as well as those who were struggling financially. The development of redlining strangled the flow of economic resources into black neighborhoods. This had the effect of excluding all blacks—rich, middle-class, and poor—from receiving banking funds, government funds, and insurance funding.

In the years following the blanket denial of development and improvement dollars to black American communities through redlining, those same neighborhoods fell into even greater decline.[2] "The effect of this 'redlining' was to hasten the physical decline of the city and escalate the process of the residential segregation."[3]

Although HOLC was a federal agency, its appraisal determinations were made by local mortgage brokers, bankers, and real estate professionals. In Miami, the attitudes of the businesspeople who made those determinations reflected the general outlook of the downtown civic leadership. At the time, this group was actively working to relocate blacks from downtown to the sparsely populated area to the northwest.[4]

HOLC security maps were made available to local bankers for evaluating mortgage applications. Because of this, bank loans were not available to type "D" communities. These communities were consigned to physical decay and intensified racial segregation. While some government loans were available to these areas, local financial institutions used the security maps to further strengthen their existing discriminatory loan practices.[5]

REDLINING AS A CONTINUING PRACTICE

Although the federal Fair Housing Act was instituted to outlaw the practice of redlining the nation's black neighborhoods, the practice continues in subtle and not-so-subtle ways. Recently, Nationwide Insurance was sued for practicing redlining of black neighborhoods when John Askin, former tackle for the New England Patriots and the Cleveland Browns, joined the Louisville, Kentucky, sales force. In 1993, Askin proposed opening up a satellite office with some former teammates in Louisville's predominantly black West End. Nationwide turned down the request, stating the area was not in its target market.[6] Askin was given a map with an "X" marked through the neighborhood and the words "waste of time."[7]

At least a dozen lawsuits and complaints have been filed against Nationwide across the U.S., alleging the insurance giant has engaged in a pattern of geographic discrimination—that is, redlining. Nationwide's redlining policies, according to housing groups, virtually eliminates the opportunity for people in older-home and minority neighborhoods to get high-quality insurance coverage. Some lawsuits allege that Nationwide does not enforce these guidelines for white homeowners.[8]

Fair-housing groups say that Nationwide isn't alone in denying development funds to black communities. Complaints have also been lodged against Allstate, State Farm, and American Family Insurance.[9]

BANKING AND THE BLACK AMERICAN COMMUNITY

Critics forget that white communities have benefited from development funds that have been unavailable to black communities. Funds have historically been denied to black communities for purchasing and improving homes, for bankrolling businesses, for education, for civic improvements, and for much more.

Legislation is in place to address redlining and other methods of denying economic strength to blacks. However, one still wonders what is being done to support the economy recovery needed to reverse the effects of this practice.

Redlining is not the only economic device used historically to keep black communities in a weakened state. Many laws have been enacted since the abolition of slavery for the purpose of subjugating the black race. Laws have been implemented and changed to make sure that America's blacks would never have the opportunity to compete on an equal playing field.

Even after slavery, freedom continued to be an elusive dream, because a kind of slavery continued that was tied to economic freedom and dignity. According to black historian Claud Anderson,

Being free for a black person meant being quasi-free. A black was free as long as he could prove he was free. And even then he had only a marginally greater choice concerning how he lived compared to his enslaved brethren. In 1841, while Solomon Northrup lamented the terrible conditions of more than four million black slaves, approximately 386,290 quasi-free blacks throughout the North were being subjected to 'Jim Crow' practices, a multiplicity of local ordinances and social sanctions that prohibited them from sharing fully in an affluent American society. They were forced to live in poverty and social decay. In the shadows of the American dream, blacks' freedom was little more than a cruel and sadistic joke.[10]

JIM CROW AND ECONOMIC SLAVERY

Throughout this nation's history, laws were passed that were designed to keep blacks from rising to economic equality. In 1642, the Carolina Trade Law barred blacks from the trades. In 1702, Virginia enacted the Public Office Law to prohibit blacks from holding public office. Black Americans were impeded from holding public meetings and developing a sense of community through the Virginia Anti-Assembly Law passed in 1723.

Later, in 1809, the Congressional Mail Law excluded blacks from carrying U.S. mail. The Louisiana Jury Law of 1816 provided that no black could testify against a white. And in 1819, the Missouri Literacy Law forbade blacks from assembling or teaching black slaves to read or write. In 1827, the Florida voting law restricted voting to whites only.

In the 1857 Dred Scott decision, blacks were dehumanized and disenfranchised. In 1868, the Southern Black Codes deprived blacks of the right to vote and hold public office, and in 1883, long after the Emancipation Proclamation, the Civil Rights Law of 1875 was severely limited by the Supreme Court, which challenged the constitutionality of giving free blacks equal rights.[11]

Those are just a few examples of the vast number of state laws that together formed an efficient system that for hundreds of years hindered blacks in this country from fair economic and political competition with whites.

Millions of black people in this country have not gotten and will not get the opportunities they need to achieve their full potential in life unless we do something to make those opportunities available. Society cannot and will not provide the opportunities black people need to succeed. We must create those opportunities for ourselves.

Just as those who went before us opened doors for us, those of us who have achieved some level of success must work to open even more doors for those who will come behind us. If banks won't lend money to black Americans, we should create our own banks and put our own money into them. If some corporations won't hire us, then we don't have to continue supporting their businesses. Black Americans as a community wield enormous financial power. If we would unite and work for the community as a whole, pooling our resources and our talent, we wouldn't have to suffer the indignities that many individual blacks suffer on a regular basis.

Just this kind of united undertaking, in fact, has already been attempted. Let's take a look at this amazing effort.

FREEDMAN'S BANK AND TRUST COMPANY

I discovered a fascinating footnote to black economic history in the story of the Freedman's Bank and Trust Company. It was a bank started by ex-slaves, chartered on March 3, 1865, during the Reconstruction period following the Civil War. Its purpose was to create a "leg up" from the poverty of slavery into the middle class.[12]

The Freedman's Bank spawned thriving branch banks in scores of Southern cities and succeeded through the many meager deposits of newly freed black men and women.

That brief success was destroyed by white speculators and real estate developers from Washington who used the bank's funds to launch bad investments. The investment failures destroyed nine years of steady, fruitful growth. Investors who were former slaves lost their life savings.[13]

During the Civil War, payday for both black and white troops had become a time of reckless extravagance when gamblers, prostitutes, and confidence men descended on the camps to fleece the troops. To counter this, Union officials attempted an allotment system to have deductions from their pay sent monthly to designated banks. The plan worked well in some states, but it was not established by all. In addition, many black soldiers distrusted white banks.

An ambitious and practical venture to help the soldiers was presented. On August 27, 1864, the Beauford (South Carolina) Military Savings Bank was created. Promoters of the bank argued that with the current high cotton prices and large bounty payment, it was the duty of even the humblest person to save for his future well-being.

The bank was to be a secure place of deposit, yield a fair rate of interest, and support the government by investing in

United States bonds. Black soldiers and some civilians responded enthusiastically.[14]

One year after its inception, the South Carolina Freedman's Savings Bank held in its safe $180,000 almost exclusively in funds from people who just a few months before had been propertyless slaves. This was at a time when $5 could purchase a week's worth of kitchen supplies, so you can see what a fortune this represented.[15]

In today's dollars, the $75,000 bounty received in 1865 by a black soldier as a payment for fighting would equal $816,588.89—a veritable fortune. The $180,000 in revenues collected in the first year of the banking venture would equal $1,959,813.34 in today's money, adjusted for inflation.[16]

These were enormous sums of money, enough to purchase land and elevate a person into a higher economic status.

LITTLE FOXES IN THE BANK'S CHARTER

Initially, Congress enacted the bank's charter. Its stated purpose was to instruct newly freed slaves in the virtues of work, thrift, and self-sufficiency. The founders intended to bring former slaves into the mainstream of working-class America. The bank would not be a charity, but it would promote the virtue of hard work that would in turn lead to self-respect.[17]

Other savings institutions in the North had been formed as benevolent and philanthropic efforts of the rich and influential to aid the worthy poor. Congress determined that the Freedman's Bank would be an ordinary savings bank with no special privileges. Yet some leaders felt that establishing such an institution nationwide reached beyond the largesse of government, and they stipulated that the bank could be located only in Washington, D.C.

Later, this stipulation was challenged, and branches went up around the country, especially in the South where ex-slaves tended to live. The legality of this structure troubled the trustees, as the original intent of Congress had been clear in restricting the offices to the nation's capital.

Eventually, the banks enjoyed substantial participation at various levels by blacks. After some jockeying back and forth, ex-slaves were eventually placed in administrative and leadership roles together with whites. Black advisory boards were also set up to oversee the business under the oversight of whites.

In less than two years after it was founded, 22 branches were established in 13 states and the District of Columbia. The trustees and officers had created a miniature financial empire, more impressive in its extensiveness than in its fiscal strength.[18]

Overreaching and Overextending

Rapid expansion created massive organizational problems. Staffs were largely untrained. Communications between branches was poor. Many branches in the Deep South had no contact at all with the central office. Only one inspector existed to oversee the efficient and correct implementation of business. Primary positions were held on a voluntary basis, so essential business often had to take a backseat to work that paid.[19] Many of the banks reported having trouble balancing their books.

In addition, those who formed the bank expected that the large bounty claims paid by the Reconstruction government to Negro soldiers or their relatives would be deposited at the Freedman's Bank, but such was not the case. The government ruled that these funds would be deposited in the U.S. Treasury. Only when a soldier was paid could the bank expect to receive his funds.

Eventually the bank failed due to gross mismanagement, over-expansion, loans that were never repaid, and financial abuse. Some bankers abused the system by lending money to their white friends who reneged on the notes. One national bank that had borrowed half a million dollars from Freedman's never paid it back, but instead sent Freedman's non-negotiable receipts. Riddled with abuses, the bank began to collapse around 1870.

As news of the faltering funds emerged, investors began a run on the bank, seeking to collect their money while it was still possible. Many of these people had built up their life savings with deposits of nickels, dimes, and pennies. Needless to say, a lot of people never got their money back.

Frederick Douglass was later brought in to the picture to see if he could recapture and rebuild the scandalous Freedman's Bank. He was named president of the bank, put $10,000 of his own money into Freedman's, and started shutting branches down. Douglass had great intentions, but Freedman's Bank was so far in the red that he could not successfully accomplish his task.

During his tenure, Douglass uncovered massive fraud and abuse by both blacks and whites. However, upon leaving the broken institution, he commented that Freedman's Bank was "the black man's cow and the white man's milk," referring to the theft of funds by white investors.[20]

Those who lost their life savings never got it back. But the possibility of creating a banking system sensitive to the needs of the black communities in this country is very real and very possible.

I've detailed this dramatic economic effort in the black community to suggest that it's time that community leaders begin thinking outside the box. Black Americans as a community wield enormous financial power. If banks won't lend money to blacks, we should create our own banks and put our own money in them.

Several groups around the country are joining together to do just that, in an attempt to financially underwrite a resurgence of business and growth within black American communities. I am involved in just such an effort, and it's enjoying some degree of success.

EMPOWERING OUR COMMUNITIES

Creating a community-based banking system looks easy enough to do on paper. But over the years I have discovered that there are risks involved in providing financial support to try to help people build businesses. A few years back, I was working on a project in which a million dollars was needed to start a community bank. A colleague of mine put my name on the line for a million dollars without my consent. After learning of his commitment, I called him up and said, "Man, I don't have a million dollars to give to this right now."

He said, "Don't worry about it. We have a way to get it." Well "we" didn't have a way to get it, and I had to come up with it.

We started our community banking project in Knoxville, Tennessee, and called it Urban Hope. Now we're working on an extension of it in Green Bay, Wisconsin. We provide a business training program to teach entrepreneurs how to create a business plan and obtain grants and community funds to get started. We have a good relationship with the banking community in Green Bay, which has encouraged our efforts.

We decided to go to Green Bay because it was such a small city that we felt we might find a strong base of support, which we have done. It may be more difficult to accomplish our objectives in a larger city, unless all the community leaders come together and work together. Therefore, right now we're focusing our efforts on medium-sized population centers and smaller rural areas where we can have the greatest impact. Urban Hope has enjoyed wide support in Green Bay, with the former governor of Wisconsin, Tommy Thompson, helping in the obtaining of a $300,000 grant to launch the project.

One of the factors in Green Bay that I'm most proud of is the way in which the entire community has gotten behind it. Everyone from state and local government officials to business people to bankers—everybody is involved and committed. Politicians, including Carol Kelso from the state Legislature, and bankers, including Peter Platten and John Underwood, have supported this project and thereby made an amazing impact on the local economy. Owners of auto repair shops, beauty shops, restaurants, home-based businesses, and other businesses have been empowered to succeed through this cooperative effort.

Over the past five years we've been able to help over 250 businesses. But our success has been due to the collaboration of all these government agencies and local groups. In every community, it will take this kind of collaborative effort in order to make a real impact.

IMPARTING KNOWLEDGE

A major hurdle that must be overcome in our communities is the longstanding "employee" mindset of the black community. Too few black Americans dream of launching their own businesses and creating their own avenues of wealth. Most see income as a benefit of working for someone else. Working for others is a powerful tool to learn about a particular business, but an employee should always look for the day when he or she can launch into an independent enterprise. If we work in a store, we should consider owning our own store one day.

One crippling factor for potential black entrepreneurs is that few understand the process of establishing a business. They don't even know how to create a business plan. Granddaddy was a slave, daddy was a truck driver, and our potential business owner lacks the role models who might have instilled the values and acumen needed to launch out independently.

To address this need, our organization is committed to teaching potential business owners how to create a business plan. In addition, we are also imparting an understanding of the tax laws, accounting procedures, and bookkeeping required to successfully maintain a thriving business.

Teaching basic financial wisdom is vital if our communities are going to succeed and thrive economically. It's not uncommon in our neighborhoods to find poor kids who pay $150 for sneakers but who are never taught to invest in their future. Someone needs to tell them that a $30 pair of sneakers is just as good as the expensive ones, and they can deposit the $120 that's left over into a savings account. Fighting the barrage of advertising messages and replacing it with good business sense will be no easy task, but it must be done.

I'd like to see the community of believers take a role in imparting business principles. We have business people sitting in our churches week after week, but they are underutilized as teachers and encouragers. Our churches view those individuals as a source of funds but seldom think any further than that. Business people should have a greater platform in order to benefit our communities with their wisdom. For instance, if a woman in my congregation has earned millions as an investor, she should have an opportunity to share how she accomplished such an impressive feat. She's earned the right to be heard and respected.

COMMUNITY EMPOWERMENT

Recently, a wealthy Jewish friend and I were discussing this vision for community empowerment. He said, "Reggie, I want to help as much as possible, because I believe your problems are my problems. This isn't just a black problem; it's an American problem. If you provide me with a strategic plan for community empowerment, I'll put my money into it. I'll do anything I can; I'll give my time and my resources."

I don't take a salary for my work in Green Bay. My goal is to see our communities change regardless of whether or not I benefit financially. My Jewish friend is not alone in his desire to help out; many individuals will join hands with us to help us initiate real change and genuine economic recovery in black communities, once our efforts start making an impact.

We will have achieved our goal when poverty levels decline. When the heads of households are able to make a decent living and when families can rear their children without lack, then our combined efforts will have made a difference.

ENDNOTES

1. John Little, "A History of Redlining," Community-Based Economic Development Homepage: www.shadow.net/johnl.

2. Ibid.

3. Ibid.

4. Ibid.

5. Ibid.

6. Christine Dugas, "Serving Blacks Brings Reprisals by Nationwide Insurance," *USA Today*, March 1997.

7. Ibid.

8. Ibid.

9. Ibid.

10. Claud Anderson, *Black Labor, White Wealth* (Bethesda, MD: PowerNomics Corporation of America Publishers, 1994), p. 11.

11. Ibid., 223-229.

12. Carl R. Osthaus, *Freedmen, Philanthropy, and Fraud* (Urbana, IL: University of Illinois Press, 1976), p. 1.

13. Ibid., p. 2.

14. Ibid., pp. 2-3.

15. Ibid., p. 3.

16. The Inflation Calculator: morgan@westegg.com.

17. Osthaus, p. 10.

18. Ibid., p. 21.

19. Ibid., p. 25.

20. Ibid., p. 1.

CHAPTER SEVEN

IT TAKES TEAMWORK
TO MAKE THE DREAM WORK

Community

---

*Our nettlesome task is to discover how to organize
our strength into compelling power.*
–Martin Luther King Jr.

WHEN THE GREEN BAY PACKERS WON the Super Bowl XXXI against New England in January 1997, it was the team's first championship in 29 years. It was exciting when quarterback Brett Favre and I were declared two of the biggest stars in the game. It was also exciting to complete three sacks for a 35-21 win. But the excitement and sense of achievement of that victory paled in comparison to what I considered to be one of Green Bay's greatest accomplishments, one of which I am most proud. That is the successful achievement of genuine teamwork—teamwork that let us realize a dream, a dream that is still working.

That sense of teamwork was illustrated by the fact that everyone got a Super Bowl ring after we won—everyone. The equipment managers, trainers, our wives, our kids, the guy who sold tickets, the kid who cut the grass, and even the secretaries and receptionists at the front desk all got Super Bowl rings to commemorate our victory. And it truly was *our* victory—we all won it together, because we were a team.

All those people loved our team so much that they became as much a part of it as the players and coaches on the field. Everyone worked together, united by a common purpose and cause. For me, it was football's finest hour.

I'm convinced that our ability to work together was the key to winning the championship. It wasn't just something that happened, however. We *learned* to work together, which made the victory that much sweeter.

One of the things I learned is that you can have all the talent in the world, but if you don't have everyone on the same page, and if you don't have men out there who don't care who gets the glory, you won't reach the height of your ability. I am very grateful for winning the championship in Green Bay, because I was able to experience the dramatic impact of true teamwork. All we cared about was winning the championship.

Football taught me some valuable lessons about life, about what it takes to make success happen. Success in our communities is no different. If we became determined to work together for the overall success of our communities and our people, there's no telling how far we could go. Teamwork in our communities could provide a legacy to pass on to generations we'll never see, and it could make an impact that might change destiny of countless people. But that kind of impact, and that kind of teamwork, doesn't come about in a day. It takes the team's total dedication and commitment to the task for as long as it takes to bring about success.

Learning to Be a Team

In his second or third year in the NFL, Brett Favre was nowhere near the top of his game. He had become discouraged by constant criticism from the press and the community. I sat down with him and told him I believed in him. I said, "Brett, as much as people get on you, I'm for you. I know you make a lot of mistakes, but there are a lot of good things that you do. Those are the things I see. When losing starts to hurt, that's when this team is going to start winning."

It took a lot of work, but we were finally playing better, and eventually we made it to the NFC championship game against Dallas. We lost that game by a score of 38 to 28, and when we got on the bus to leave the stadium Brett cried. Losing was starting to hurt, and I realized our turning point had come. I took a look at Brett's face, and I knew deep inside that we were going to win the next Super Bowl.

Green Bay was undergoing the painful process of becoming a true team. We started to work together very well. Several new players made a big difference, but even more important was the growing sense of community we were enjoying. We were becoming a tightly knit family. There was no jealousy and no jockeying for position; we were having a good time playing together as a team. Even complaints were handled in a productive manner. We had a great year.

Eventually, each player put aside his ego. We became united in one purpose: to win the Super Bowl. Our desire to finally beat Dallas unified us and sharpened our commitment to each other. We truly became one family—a community of players, coaches, wives, kids, groundskeepers, and other support staff united in one purpose. Together, we made a commitment to one another.

As a team, we began to realize that if Brett, our quarterback, could get to the top of his game, then winning would become a lot easier for all of us. Eventually, Brett got there.

You know, one of the team's greatest attributes during that time of growth was the lack of jealousy. I really don't think I encountered one player who was jealous of someone else. That absence of jealousy made the difference in our whole championship team. Free from the negative energy that accompanies this sabotaging emotion, the team could rise quickly and powerfully to its full potential.

When we won the Super Bowl in 1997 against the New England Patriots, it proved that teamwork does make the dream work. We didn't march out on that field as individual star athletes. We came out as a unit, one united, powerful, committed, honed instrument that was ready to play.

A VISION OF COMMUNITY

I believe that one of the reasons that our communities—whether black or any other—haven't attained the hope of their promise is that we've never pulled together in the same direction as a people. We've come together, but we haven't laid down our personal agendas, personal ambitions, and personal goals to embrace a dream that's bigger than all of us together as individuals. The whole *is* greater than the sum of its parts. We can maximize the strength of each individual by incorporating that person into a team.

The Green Bay Packers were unable to come into unity until we all held the same vision. Proverbs 29:18 says, "Where there is no vision, the people perish, but he that keepeth the law, happy is he" (KJV). If our vision as a community is not based on God's law, then in some ways, we have no vision at all. It's the same with a dream. If our dream is not based on building community, there is no dream at all. The concept of unity through God's Word is at the core of everything I believe about community.

Even in the Bible, the visions and dreams God gave to leaders were related to the success or the failure of community. God didn't call Moses for Moses. God called Moses for His people. When we realize that the Messiah has called each one of us to use our lives to benefit and edify His people, then we will begin to build a true community.

Often when we talk about our dreams and visions we're speaking solely of ourselves as individuals. We have no sense of community in our dreams and visions. We have no conviction of the purpose of our lives with respect to our impact on those around us. We think in terms of what *I* will do, what *I* will achieve, and how *I* will go about achieving it. We must come to see our purpose and vision in a larger perspective. The meaning and value of our lives must be understood in a broader sense— in the sense of community.

The purposes of our lives much reach beyond the scope of our individuality. Only when we lose our lives in a greater cause beyond the borders of our own self-interest will we discover the joyful awareness of our true significance and purpose. We must sow the meaning of our lives into the greater promise of community in order to grasp the purpose of our lives and see it fulfilled.

Many of us believe that we understand Martin Luther King Jr.'s dream because we've heard his powerful speeches and listened to the eloquence of his words. But King had much to say about community, and to a significant degree, his dream was built upon a concept of community, which he wrote about while studying to receive his Ph.D. at Boston University. It was there that this great leader formed his understanding of nonviolence, Christian morality, and the beloved community.

KING'S BELOVED COMMUNITY

King framed the passion and activities of his life around a concept he called the beloved *community*. "The classic expression of King's attitude toward community lies in his definition and use of the Greek concept *agape* (pronounced "ah-GAH-pay"), 'love,' defined by him in 1958 as "a willingness to go to any length to restore community."[1]

The source for this interpretation of love is the Swedish theologian Anders Nygren who, in his classic work *Agape and Eros*, wrote: "*Agape* does not recognize value, but creates it. *Agape* loves and imparts value by loving. The man who is loved by God has no value in himself; what gives him value is precisely the fact that God loves him."[2]

King believed that mankind, as lover and thereby creator of value, creates the beloved community. According to his interpretation of *agape*, it is in being loved that you receive value, and it is in selflessly loving others that you impart value to them, which makes the beloved community possible.[3] *Agape*—selfless, giving love—is a key to bringing about King's dream of community.

The first appearance of King's beloved community concept is found in his stated goals concerning the Montgomery bus boycott in April 1957. He writes that the goal was "reconciliation; the end [was] redemption; the end [was] creation of the beloved community."[4]

American theologian Walter Rauschenbush may have influenced King's social gospel more than any other religious leader did. He argued that the primary purpose of Christianity was to "transform human society into the kingdom of God."[5]

King's concept often sounds similar to what Rauschenbush called "true human community" or "righteous community." The concept expresses a "progressive reign of love in human affairs which is best expressed in 'service to others.'"[6]

King ultimately rejected Rauschenbush's social gospel and went on to develop his own concept of the beloved community. Concerning his experience with Rauschenbush's concepts, he said:

> I was immediately influenced by the social gospel [at Crozer Theological Seminary in 1950] as a method to eliminate social evil....I read Rauschenbusch's *Christianity and the Social Crisis*....[But] I felt that he had fallen victim to the nineteenth century "cult of inevitable progress" which led to an unwarranted optimism concerning human nature. Moreover, he came perilously close to identifying the Kingdom of God with a particular social and economic system—a temptation which the church should never give in to.[7]

The "beloved community," while rooted in the Protestant tradition, remains King's own unique contribution to a new social gospel aimed at ridding the world of social evils.[8] Later, he would call his "beloved community" the "broken community." In a speech to the National Press Club in Washington, D.C., in July 1962, King spoke of the relationship between violence and "the broken community." He said:

> I feel that this way of nonviolence is vital because it is the only way to reestablish the broken community. It is the method which seeks to implement the just law by appealing to the conscience of the great decent majority who through blindness, fear, pride, or irrationality have allowed their consciences to sleep.[9]

ACTS OF LOVE AND THE BELOVED COMMUNITY

That sleeping community conscience can be awakened through acts of love. And those acts of love are nonviolent, direct, Christian social actions:

> The nonviolent resisters can summarize their message in the following simple terms: We will take direct action against injustice without waiting for other agencies to act. We will not obey unjust laws or submit to unjust practices. We will do this peacefully, openly, cheerfully because our aim is to persuade. We adopt the means of nonviolence because our end is a community at peace with itself.[10]

For the beloved community concept to work, altruistic agape love must reign supreme. Leaders must lead on behalf of the people, never for the benefit of their own agendas or the promotion of personal privilege. Those who have must not neglect those who have not; as we invest in others, we invest in our own future.

With the Green Bay Packers, we learned that laying down personal agendas in order to take up a cause larger than ourselves as individuals was a key to success. To do so requires some measure of the agape love of which King spoke so eloquently. We need each other to win, and therefore our destinies are tied to each other's. King said:

> The universe is so structured that things do not quite work out rightly if men are not diligent in their concern for others. The self cannot be self without other selves. I cannot reach fulfillment without thou. Social psychologists tell us that we cannot truly be persons unless we interact with other persons. All life is

interrelated. All men are caught in an inescapable network of mutuality, tied in a single garment of destiny.[11]

In 1966, in an article in *Ebony*, King repeated the goal for community that he had been seeking to identify and implement:

Only a refusal to hate or kill can put an end to the chain of violence in the world and lead us toward a community where men can live together without fear. Our goal is to create a beloved community, and this will require a qualitative change in our souls as well as a qualitative change in our lives.[12]

Nevertheless, King didn't suggest that the rights and privileges of individuals should be submerged and forgotten beneath the power of a greater community. That would be a kind of modern socialism. King fought for the rights of the individual, believing that a true Christian could find the balance between altruistic love, nonviolent change, and empowerment of individuals through the greater benefits provided by the whole—provided by the beloved community.

A BOLD COMMITMENT TO COMMUNITY

King was committed to community, and he gave his life for that commitment. The Bible says, "Greater love has no man than this, that a man lay down his life for his friends" (Jn. 15:13 RSV). King's altruistic love for community was underscored by his sacrificial death.

He believed in us, too. He was certain that we could rise up and achieve his dream of the beloved community. As he accepted the Nobel Peace Price in 1964, he said:

I accept this award today with an abiding faith in America and an audacious faith in the future of mankind. I refuse to accept the idea that the "isness" of man's present nature makes him morally incapable of reaching up for the eternal "oughtness" that forever confronts him....I believe that unarmed truth and unconditional love will have the final word in reality. This is why *temporarily defeated* is stronger than *evil triumphant.*[13]

REACHING FOR THE BELOVED COMMUNITY

King's dream was not empty, meaningless, overly idealistic rhetoric. His dream wasn't lost at his death. This dream for a community is real and possible if we choose to make the dream a reality. But first we must accept that it will take teamwork to make the dream work. We must make our own path—and not just individually. We must work to carve out a way for others. We must reject the consumerism and greed that promotes selfishness.

When I succeed, I need to be committed to pulling my brothers and sisters up with me. If I'm living well, I need to find ways to make sure my brothers are living well, without allowing them to take advantage of my kindness. We must teach people how to work so they can be a blessing to those around them. I must seek to discover how I can be a part of God blessing the black community and this nation at large.

The government alone cannot change the course of America. It will take the contribution of one family joining with other families in order to change their community. Each individual and each community will have to take full control of their own destinies rather than rely on religious and political leaders with misguided agendas. We must come to the full understanding that no religious or political law can transcend God's law.

When we awaken and embrace our destiny as a united community of individuals, we will discover celebration and joy.

What Happened to the Celebration?

When we come together in community there should be celebration, for communities were created, in part, in order to celebrate themselves—to rejoice in their own ongoing existence. The ancient Israelites held big parties when they observed certain Sabbaths and festivals. They celebrated every month during the new moon. They also had three major feasts, together with their monthly celebrations, which seems like a commitment to celebration to me.

When I was growing up I always looked forward to getting together with our extended family on the 4th of July. My uncles would grill chicken, and we'd fill up on fried chicken, sweet potato pie, greens, and lots of other delicious foods. The children would run through the yards while the adults sat and talked and enjoyed each other's company. We always looked forward to the community celebration because we knew we were going to have a good time.

Let's not let go of our celebration of beloved community. Let's determine to get together often to build relationships, communicate with one another, and get to know one another. The joy we will receive from celebrating the bonds of community is like a medicine. There is power in celebrating together. It enhances the spirit of community. Too many people in our communities exist in isolation, and we've forgotten to enjoy the presence of one another.

We live in a pressure-cooker society. Our jobs, our families, our crises—all of these things work together to create stresses that rob us of the joy we should be finding in our relationships.

What a pleasure it is to cut loose with your friends and have a great time. Celebrating community and the relationships around us keeps us from disintegrating and becoming dysfunctional.

Recently, we had Sara's dad and mom, my cousin, and their in-laws over to our house. We played cards, and the kids went swimming. I sat back and looked at my cousin and thought, *I miss this. This is fun. When I was younger we used to do this all the time.*

RELATIONSHIPS AND COMMUNITY

For the past few years I have become increasingly committed to community by building relationships. A group of friends comes together regularly for fellowship. The social gatherings have been fun for me. We've had cookouts, and we sit and talk about what's going on in our lives.

That's the way life is supposed to be. We should feel comfortable enough to go over to each other's homes and sit down and relax, share our dreams, our feelings, our hopes, and our disappointments. We were created to be people bonded together in community. We were meant to be a team.

Once a friend confided that he enjoyed coming over because he felt comfortable with us, just as if he were at home. He told me he was able to hear some of the difficult things I had to say to him because he knew he was surrounded by friends who cared about him.

It may not happen all at once, but I believe that we can change the course of our history. We can join hands together and hearts together, and we can become a community of people bonded to one another once more—committed to the whole, which is greater than the sum of the parts. Once again, we can choose to believe in one another, trust one another, and lay aside our own selfish interests for the sake of the beloved community. We can't do it alone, but with teamwork, we can determine to make the dream work.

Endnotes

1. A. L. Herman, *Community, Violence, and Peace: Aldo Leopold, Mohandas K. Gandhi, Martin Luther King, Jr., and Gautama the Buddha in the Twenty-first Century* (Albany, NY: State University of New York Press, 1999): www.netLibrary.com.

2. Ibid.

3. Ibid.

4. Ibid.

5. Ibid.

6. Ibid.

7, Ibid.

8. Ibid.

9. Ibid.

10. Ibid.

11. Ibid.

12. Ibid.

13. The King Center; the Beloved Community: www.thekingcenter.com/mlk/bio.html.

CHAPTER EIGHT

RED AND YELLOW BLACK AND WHITE

Racial Unity

I have a dream that one day on the red hills of Georgia, sons of former slaves and sons of former slave-owners will be able to sit down together at the table of brotherhood.
–Martin Luther King Jr.

RECENTLY, I DELIVERED A SPEECH in Arizona to a group of white businessmen seeking their support in bringing economic recovery to the black community. I was genuinely amazed at their enthusiasm and readiness to help. The standard wisdom within the black community is that whites won't support black causes. Yet I realized as I looked into the faces of these very successful, influential individuals that they were eager to help.

It's imperative that we in the black community stop seeing white men and women as the enemy. They are not. Racism is the enemy, and it can be found in both the white and black communities. Hatred is the enemy. Poverty, oppression, lack—these things are the enemies of mankind, of both blacks and whites.

Much of what we hear from the media appears to continually stir up racial division, old wounds, distrust, and resentment. Less frequently do we hear political figures working to heal wounds and build racial bridges. The media seems poised to air anything that intensifies racial anger in the black community or fear of blacks in the white community.

When have you ever heard the media talk about whites who have paid a price to help the black community—or vice versa? Not often. Instead, both communities are painted in ways that are divisive and inflammatory and do little to promote harmony or good will.

Martin Luther King Jr. was confronted with unimaginably vicious racial hatred. White racists bombed his home, and he was shot at, threatened, beaten, and jailed. Finally, he was murdered in one supreme act of racial rage. A statement he made just days before his murder indicated that he sensed his death was imminent. Nevertheless, King refused to give in to hatred. He said, "In using the term 'white man' I am seeking to describe in general terms the Negro's adversary. It is not meant to encompass all white people. There are millions who have morally risen above prevailing prejudices."

In the thick of racial turbulence during the Montgomery bus boycott, some whites resisted the temptation to go along with the white racists. While some white employers fired black workers that took part in the boycott, some white women indirectly aided the boycott by driving their maids and babysitters to and from work. Many white men became angry about this, but the women refused to stop.[1]

King's dream went beyond economic and social vindication for black men and women. He dreamed of social harmony in a nation where blacks and whites would coexist in an atmosphere of mutual respect and dignity. He saw the possibility of a beautiful symphony of brotherhood. He said,

> With this faith we will be able to hew out of the mountain of despair a stone of hope. With this faith we will

be able to transform the jangling discords of our nation into a beautiful symphony of brotherhood.[2]

Rosa Parks ignited the Montgomery bus boycott on December 1, 1955, when she refused to relinquish her seat at the front of the "colored section" of the segregated Cleveland Avenue bus to a white man. Rosa affirmed King's desire to seek racial harmony. She said:

> Dr. King was scheduled to return to Detroit on April 11, and I was sure I would have an opportunity to meet with him then, but he was assassinated on April 4.
>
> The hurt I felt was almost unbearable when I heard of his death. It left me numb. It was almost as if I had been shot myself. His life and his leadership had meant so much to me that it is still difficult to describe what a personal loss it was.
>
> I, along with many others, have accepted the challenge to fulfill his dream by fulfilling my own. The "beloved community" he often spoke of is one of respect and opportunity for all people.[3]

King's concept of the beloved community didn't end at the borders of the black community. He saw a symphony of communities, much like the layers of a score of music. Each community would operate in peace within itself, and then those communities would work together with other communities in harmony and peace. His concept of brotherhood stretched beyond the brotherhood of men and women of one race and color. He saw the shining possibility of a genuine brotherhood of mankind.

King wasn't the only individual who dreamed of racial unity. Many whites and blacks throughout history have paid a great price to build bridges across the racial divide.

WHITES WHO DIED SEEKING RACIAL JUSTICE

An important aspect of often-ignored black American history is the sacrifice that God-fearing whites have made to the cause of racial justice. History is filled with those who paid a price seeking racial unity.

Thaddeus Stevens, a white man who lived during the 1800s, maintained a law practice in Lancaster, Pennsylvania. He devoted his life to the cause of equality for blacks and at his death insisted on being buried in a cemetery with blacks. That was a radical gesture that declared his sense of brotherhood with all of God's children.

James Reeb was a white minister who was beaten to death by a group of white racists for participating in the Civil Rights march in Selma, Alabama, in 1965.[4]

Two of the most dramatic accounts of white abolitionists who paid a great price for racial freedom involve Elijah Lovejoy and John Brown. Let's take a look at the lives of these men.

ELIJAH LOVEJOY

Elijah Lovejoy, a white abolitionist, was shot and killed on November 7, 1837, in Alton, Illinois, because of his anti-slavery efforts there. Lovejoy, a Presbyterian minister, was the editor of an abolitionist newspaper famous for its anti-slavery editorials. He wrote, "Slavery as it now exists among us must cease to exist. There can be no doubt on this subject; God and man…alike forbid its perpetuity."[5]

Racist mobs destroyed several of his printing presses in opposition to his antislavery messages. Although he feared for his own safety as well as the safety of his wife and newborn son, Lovejoy refused to stop speaking out against slavery. His efforts influenced wealthy supporters like Winthrop Gilman, owner of the Godfrey & Gilman warehouse, and Royal Weller, owner of a shoe store.

An August 1836 letter written to his mother revealed his courage and character:

> You ask, Are you discouraged? I answer promptly, no…I have pled the cause of the poor and oppressed; I have maintained the rights of humanity. For these things I have seen my family scattered, my office broken up…have been loaded with execrations, had all manner of evil spoken falsely against me, and finally had my life threatened. Yet none of these things moves me from my purpose; by the grace of God I will not, I will not forsake my principles. I will maintain and propagate them with all the means He puts into my hands. The cry of the oppressed has entered not only into my ears, but into my soul so that while I live I cannot hold my peace. Such as I have, I give freely— my time, my energy, the best years of my life, some little ability, and a good deal of zeal. These I give, and bless God for the opportunity, to so holy a cause. I may not live to see its success. I may even die—though most unworthy—its victim and its martyr. Yet it will ultimately succeed, and that too at no distant day. I am as well assured as I am that there is a God in heaven who sits on a throne of righteousness.[6]

Religious leaders decried his antislavery message. Lovejoy believed that those who refused to fight against slavery were fighting against God. He denounced those who "preached against intemperance and Sabbath breaking, against covetousness and murder, yet passed over slavery in silence."

Lovejoy also stated, "If I could hold my peace on this subject with a clear conscience, I would most assuredly do it. But I cannot, and I am sure you do not ask or wish a Christian to connive at what he believes to be a sin, for the sake of popularity."[7]

When the mob showed up intending to gun down Lovejoy at Godfrey & Gilman's warehouse, Lovejoy declared: "We must fight it out, if necessary, to the bitter end. I, for one, am willing and ready to lay down my life."[8]

On the night of November 7, 1837, 150 angry, hate-filled men wanted to destroy Lovejoy's new printing press inside the Godfrey & Gilman warehouse. Lovejoy and his supporters grabbed their rifles and refused to back down. But the mob set the building on fire and shot Lovejoy five times. The press was destroyed, and it seemed that evil had triumphed. However, in the end more abolitionists of both races joined the cause.[9]

Elijah Lovejoy burned to death. He was buried on November 9, 1837, his thirty-fifth birthday.

Through his death, Elijah Lovejoy proved he was a friend of justice, equality, and righteousness.

BATTLE AT HARPERS FERRY

Hollywood rarely makes movies about black issues that portray whites who have supported black causes. Most of the movies we see show whites beating and brutalizing blacks, which evokes anger. Yet history has proven that there have been many righteous whites who have been deeply committed to justice for both races.

Frederick Douglass said that John Brown, a white man, cared more about black people than he himself did. Brown died fighting for the freedom of black slaves. Brown's wife and children fought for the cause as well.[10]

This white revolutionary believed he was ordained by God to help free the black race from enslavement. With a party of 21, including his sons, daughters, and five blacks, Brown entered West Virginia and captured the town of Harpers Ferry, seized the U.S. armory, and freed 50 slaves.[11]

According to historian Claud Anderson, this one revolutionary act was the match that ignited the fires of racial revolution. He said,

> More than any other white before or since, Brown confronted the issue of black liberation forthrightly at a high personal cost. He sacrificed, not just his own life, but the lives of a number of his own children. With this series of revolutionary acts, the white militant almost single-handedly created the passionate emotional climate that led to the Civil War.[12]

People may not agree with John Brown's militant revolutionary methods, but his courage and commitment to racial equality was beyond dispute. It was a sad day for many free and enslaved blacks when they knelt and wept over the body of John Brown as it hung from gallows in Charles Town, West Virginia, on December 2, 1859.

When Frederick Douglass paid his last respects to Brown, he made the following statement:

> Brown's struggle in the cause of freedom was superior to mine. Mine was a small light; his was a burning sun. Mine was bound by time; his stretched away to the

silent shores of eternity. As a black man, I am willing to speak for the slave; John Brown, a white man, was willing to die for the slave. How do you explain this?[13]

The story of John Brown provides another vital perspective on American race relations. His life and the lives of so many others who stood tall against impossible odds in the fight for racial justice provides balance. Some in the Nation of Islam attempt to paint white Christians with one brush as "blued-eyed devils" who enslaved blacks. But that sweeping depiction is unfair.

Although much has been said about the motives of those who fought the Civil War, it's beyond dispute that many fought and died in this country's bloodiest war over the issue of slavery. Many brave soldiers poured their own blood on the ground in an effort to cleanse the nation's soil from its most grievous sin. We would do their memory an injustice to forget their sacrifice. Although we don't know their names, those who bled and died specifically to free the black man proved their love.

Many whites have risen up for the cause of justice and dignity for all mankind. Even in our own generation, many are willing to make great sacrifices.

An Enemy of the Human Heart

In April 1961, in the midst of Martin Luther King Jr.'s work, the Freedom Rides began. They were interstate tours of buses loaded with both black and white Civil Rights workers, boarding in Washington, D.C., and traveling through the South. These tours turned frightening as both blacks and whites witnessed gross bloodshed.

Freedom rider James Zerg, a student at the University of Wisconsin, was beaten unconscious in Montgomery, Alabama. An angry mob in Anniston, Alabama, threw a bomb into a Freedom

Rides bus filled with blacks and whites, and many riders suffered injury.[14]

BRIDGING THE DIVIDE

Even so, racism continues today in many subtle and less-than-subtle ways. What can be done to bridge the racial divide between the nation's black and white communities?

White *Newsweek* journalist Tamar Jacoby asks this poignant question in her book, *Somebody Else's House*. She writes,

> The middle class has quadrupled, educational levels have soared, blacks are increasingly well represented in electoral politics and other influential realms of national life.

> Still, as I thought about my *Newsweek* researcher, I had to wonder if integration was really possible. Like a growing number of blacks in America, she was leading an integrated life, but for her this hard-won achievement seemed all but meaningless. Accomplished as she was, she still felt deeply alienated, an uncomfortable and unwelcome visitor in someone else's house.

> "I've seen plenty of physical integration," a black college student said to me a few weeks later. "That doesn't guarantee integration of the heart."[15]

How can blacks stop feeling as if they're "unwelcome visitors in someone else's house"? How do we go beyond legislative integration to the Promised Land of brotherhood of which Dr. King dreamed?

COMMUNITY BROTHERHOOD COVENANTS

I don't believe that the races will ever come to a place of true unity until we begin to make covenant as brothers. In ancient times, tribes made covenants with one another, which they then honored throughout their existence.

Covenants are a powerful biblical concept. Even God made a covenant with Abraham. Jonathan and David made a covenant together as individuals. And many ancient tribes entered into covenant together.

In making a covenant between ethnic communities, leaders of the ancient tribes would meet together to work through the various details of those covenant agreements. Long-standing hurts, old wounds, ancient anger, and enduring rage—all the issues dividing the parties would be brought to the table to be dealt with.

Terms of the covenant were based on the negotiations of the various parties. In ancient times, covenants were sealed in blood and salt was placed on the animal that was to be sacrificed. The salt symbolized the enduring nature of the covenants.

Ancient covenants were binding on all individuals. Made before the eyes of God, the covenant could not be broken. By virtue of covenant, the weight of distrust and resentment could be washed away. Tribes could begin to live as brothers, in peace and harmony.

COVENANT BROTHERS—BLACK AND WHITE

I propose that we as a black people offer to whites the opportunity to enter into covenant. As covenant brothers and sisters before God, we will vow to lay down racial sins. We will commit to one another, in the presence of God, that we will stop judging one another by the color of our skin. We will openly and publicly repent and forgive all former racial hatred.

I propose that across this great country, black and white leaders from the highest offices in the land meet publicly to enter into covenant for the people. Once these covenants are completed and the vows before God are made, we will be bound forever as true brothers in the eyes of God and in one another's eyes.

From that moment on, blacks will accept whites as their brothers. Whites will do the same for blacks. Once we enter into brotherhood covenants, we will forever honor them and hold them dear. And because we've made vows to one another before the eyes of God, I believe that He will help us to walk together in unity and peace.

I propose that racial covenants be made in every state and every community, between black churches and white. I propose that we openly and publicly declare our intention to one another and to God, that we will forever afterward be joined as brothers, black and white.

BEYOND FLESH AND BLOOD

The Bible says that our warfare is not against flesh and blood, but against powers of wickedness (Eph. 6:12). Racism's wicked power can be found in any human heart, as can the godly power of love and tolerance. Our war against racial evil must be fought in the battleground of human hearts and minds—both white and black. Only then will we rise up to grasp the King's dream: "When all God's children—black men and white men, Jews and Gentiles, Catholics and Protestants—will be able to join hands and to sing in the words of the old Negro spiritual, 'Free at last, free at last, thank God Almighty, we are free at last.' "[16]

ENDNOTES

1. Jim Haskins, *I Have a Dream* (Brookfield, CT: The Millbrook Press, 1992), p. 42.

2. Ibid., pp. 76-79.

3. Ibid., p. 10.

4. Dr. Barbara E. Edgecombe, "The Nature of Courage": www.msu.edu/user/uulansmi/beeserm/courage.htm.

5. Jim Ryun, *Heroes Among Us* (Shippensburg, PA: Destiny Image, 2002), p. 147.

6. Ibid., p. 149.

7. Ibid., p. 150.

8. Ibid., p. 147.

9. Ibid., p. 157.

10. Claud Anderson, *Dirty Little Secrets* (Bethesda, MD: PowerNomics Corporation of America Publishers, 1997), p. 21.

11. Ibid., p. 22.

12. Ibid.

13. Ibid.

14. Haskins, pp. 58-59.

15. Tamar Jacoby, *Someone Else's House* (New York: Basic Books, 1998), pp. 2-3.

16. Haskins, p. 80.

CHAPTER NINE

FRESH LEADERSHIP FOR A NEW MILLENNIUM

---

*When the history books are written in future generations,
the historians will have to pause and say, "There lived
a great people—a black people—who injected new
meaning and dignity into the veins of civilization." This
is our challenge and our overwhelming responsibility.*
—Martin Luther King Jr.

WITHOUT A GREAT QUARTERBACK, a football team simply cannot expect to win championships. At Green Bay, standing shoulder to shoulder with quarterback Brett Favre, I learned invaluable lessons about leadership.

An essential quality of leadership is recognizing that there are people on your team who hold a more important position than your own. To win the game, you must be willing to work very hard to make sure that other individuals succeed. You must work as hard to insure the success of others as you work to insure your own success. That's how I related to Favre. For me to have success, it was important that Brett succeed. My commitment to his success helped guarantee my own success.

The Green Bay Packers may not have had as much natural talent and ability as the team I played with in Philadelphia. But the Packers went to the Super Bowl and Philly did not, because the guys in Green Bay were willing to play together. They recognized that the team as a whole was more important than the individual players.

When a true leader believes in team play, he will be willing to say, "There's a guy on this team who's going to help us move in the direction we need to go. So let's get behind him and let him do it. Let's be his supporting cast." That's what I felt about Brett.

This is where some confusion comes in. We think the star player, the top gun, is the leader of the team and therefore the rest of the team must get behind him. That's not the case. The player who promotes the team concept and makes it work—the one who is rarely seen—is the true leader. There are many leaders in the trenches.

When I left Green Bay, Brett and some other players called me often to say how much they missed me on the team. Good leadership, real leadership focuses the attention on the team and not on a single individual. The team knows in its heart who its true leaders are.

New Wineskins

Genuine leadership places the team above individual needs and desires. True leadership serves. False leadership expects to be served.

I didn't feel threatened when the management at Green Bay drafted another defensive end, because I realized that I was getting older. I determined to do all I could to groom the new players to take over when I was gone. I cared about the team, and I wanted it to go on being successful, if not more successful, long after my tenure was completed. A true leader is always working to build up other leaders and advance the goals of the team.

The shining character trait of genuine leadership is a heartfelt commitment to building up and encouraging other leaders. When the black community of the new millennium enters the Promised Land of genuine economic equality, productivity, and affluence, it will be because of fresh leadership and new vision. These leaders will think beyond outdated modalities and failed initiatives. With creative ideas and servant hearts, they will take our people to the places their ancestors only dreamed of going. Men and women with fresh ideas will break the mold of the existing corporate system.

The Bible puts it this way:

> *Nor do they put new wine into old wineskins, or else the wineskins break, the wine is spilled, and the wineskins are ruined. But they put new wine into new wineskins, and both are preserved* (Matthew 9:17 NKJV).

What will these new wineskins look like? Who will these servant leaders be? They will be people of dignity, character, and excellence. Many have already advanced far ahead and led the way in business, politics, education, sports, engineering, and other fields by their own initiative, creativity, hard work, and drive. The brightness of their exceptional achievement will shine a beacon that will light a way for others to follow. Let's look at a few individuals whose lives are creating new wineskins of leadership for the black community.

SHAQUILLE O'NEAL

Efforts of professional athletes such as Shaquille O'Neal of the Los Angeles Lakers are making a difference in their communities. Recently, Shaq purchased $100 million worth of rundown homes to restore and house needy people.

This is a creative way to make a difference in people's lives. This athlete is not a political figure, and he doesn't have a widespread reputation as a businessman. But he's making a different where it matters.

Shaq is just one of many people in professional sports, business, and entertainment who have given something back to the black community. More is being accomplished by individuals like him than by political leaders—leaders who have been given resources that our communities have never seen.

NEVER FORGET THE COST

The field of sports is replete with true heroes who helped pave the way for many others to follow—men like Hank Aaron, who comported himself with dignity and grace despite threats against his life because of the color of his skin. Fans jeered racial scorn from the stands against these early sporting greats, and still these professionals maintained their focus and excellence.

Historically, black American athletes opened doors into a white-dominated society using the exceptional command of their sports and distinctive styles. They smashed negative stereotypes with achievements that brought truth into darkened minds and hearts. With the eyes of the entire world watching, Joe Louis and Jesse Owens reduced to ashes the lies of Hitler's White Supremacist regime. While the world was fearing defeat at the hands of this racist leader, black athletes flaunted victory before his face, and America cheered.

Black American athletes have proven to the world that when the black man has a chance to play, he excels. Many blacks have excelled in all fields including business, education, the arts, music, literature, and other fields as well.

Heroes who have blazed the way for us are too numerous to mention, but here are a few: Marion Motley was the first black superstar to play in the NFL. Baseball great Willie Mays was the first player to steal 30 bases and hit 30 runs in the same season. Bill White was the National League president. Tiger Wood is a young man with unique talents who has opened the sport of golf to blacks. He is the first and only black player to win golf's treasured Masters Tournament.

Athletes continue to open doors for blacks in America and throughout the world with their exceptional abilities, unique talents, and dynamic gifts. In the past, world-class black athletes have suffered the indignities of being forced to sleep in separate hotel rooms, eat in separate quarters from white players, and endure the heckling of racists in the stands. Instead of walking away, they continued to stand tall and prove to the world that they were professionals. I have a lot of respect for these black heroes—not merely for their abilities and what they did on the field but even more so for their endurance and aplomb in the face of raging hatred and bitter injustice.

Men such as John Mackey of the Baltimore Colts paid a price for all ballplayers. He fought for free agency and was blackballed from the Hall of Fame for fifteen years. He was one of the greatest tight ends that ever played football, but he has never received the recognition he deserves for what he did for the players in the courtroom.[1]

If it hadn't been for Curt Flood, baseball players would not be making the salaries they currently receive. This all-star challenged baseball's restrictive reserve clause, and his lawsuit made it to the Supreme Court. Many of the men who challenged their profession were black men. Today's athletes are being paid well because of what we did in court. Somebody had to pay the price.

Curt Flood and John Mackey never benefited financially from their challenges to the system. Those who came after them had an easier way because of their labors.

I was a litigant in a suit for free agency, and the reason that so many pro football players are getting paid much better salaries today is because of my lawsuit. I don't know if John Mackey and Curt Flood felt unappreciated, but only a few guys have ever come up to me to say thanks. Nevertheless, I didn't do it to get a thank you; I did it because it was the right thing to do.

I feel sorry for the guys who were making the league minimum of $60,000 a year but still went on strike with us. They lost a salary they could not afford to lose, and they lost their careers in sports. Now these guys are out working regular jobs. They paid big price.

And if the salaries of athletes seem high to you, consider that an athlete must earn his total life's income in his sport in far fewer years than in others professions. For instance, the average lifespan of a football player's career lasts only four year. He works his entire life to earn in four years what someone in industry might have 40 years to earn. Athletes are a part of a union, just like other union workers. Few would argue that they should have a reasonable share together with the owners in the millions of dollars created by their hard work and exceptional talent.

The athletes who paid a price have passed the ball to us. It's time for us to rise up and assume the leadership positions in all fields—business, politics, religion—that they struggled to give us. One individual who is doing just that is Valerie Daniels-Carter.

THE VALERIE DANIELS-CARTER STORY

This dedicated black American Christian and business leader owns more restaurant franchises in this country than any other individual. Valerie Daniels-Carter obtained her first Burger King franchise in Milwaukee in 1984 when she and her brother, John Daniels Jr., incorporated as V&J Foods. Ms. Daniels-Carter has since been named a "powerhouse of the new black economy" by *Black Enterprise* magazine. She runs a company with 3,500 employees and an anticipated $92 million in revenues this year. V&J Holding Companies owns 97 Pizza Hut and 41 Burger King franchises.[1]

Daniels-Carter is committed to employing godly principles in all of her business dealings. Employees who work hard benefit from profit-sharing programs, among other incentives. This great black entrepreneur is one of many highly successful individuals who are making a difference in the black community. She is not alone at the top. A growing number of black Americans are ascending at an ever-increasing rate to fill top positions in industry and government.

ROBERT JOHNSON

As owner and CEO of Black Entertainment Television, a 24-hour programming service targeting black American consumers and one of the leading black owned and operated entertainment companies in the world, Robert L. Johnson is one of the more powerful black men in America today.

Johnson was born in Hickory, Mississippi, in 1946, the ninth of 10 children born to Archie and Edna Johnson. He went on to earn a master's degree in public administration from Princeton University. Later, he moved to Washington, D.C., where he launched his career in television.[2]

Robert Johnson went on to purchase the NBA's expansion franchise in Charlotte, North Carolina, making him the first black man to own a major professional team. The purchase was estimated at $300 million. At the time of the sale, Johnson was reportedly worth $1.3 billion, placing him on the Forbes list of richest Americans.[3]

MOST POWERFUL BLACK EXECUTIVES IN AMERICA

A recent issue of *Fortune* magazine listed 50 of the most powerful black businessmen and women in American. These powerful icons of business are but a few of the seldom-heralded achievers in black America. Let's look at some of them.

Stanley O'Neal, COO of Merrill Lynch, is in one of the most powerful positions at the leading Wall Street firm. O'Neal, technically the number-two guy at the giant corporation, is essentially running the show.

Ken Chenault is CEO of American Express, which is headquartered across the street from "Ground Zero" in New York City. He is attempting to transform the giant conglomerate into a one-stop financial shop where cardholders would purchase everything from mutual funds to financial plans.

Richard Parsons is CEO of AOL Time Warner. This black American holds the top-dog position at the world's biggest media company. He said, "I always knew I'd rise to the top; it never occurred to me I couldn't."

Franklin Raines is CEO of Fannie Mae. He was a working-class kid from Seattle whose prowess on the high school debating team won him a scholarship to Harvard. In 1999, he became the first black CEO of a Fortune 500 company.

Thomas Jones is CEO of global investments, private banking, and asset management at Citigroup. Jones oversees

12,000 employees across four business units at the $112 billion operation.

Bruce Gordon is president of retail markets for Verizon. This telecom industry veteran runs the biggest business for the nation's largest phone company. Gordon's retail markets unit brings in some $25 billion in annual revenues, has 34,000 employees, and serves 33 million residential customers.

Lloyd Trotter is president and CEO of GE Industrial Systems at General Electric. Leading one of GE's major businesses, Trotter has built industrial systems into a heavyweight division that posted $6 million in revenues last year and employs 40,000 people worldwide.

Brenda Gaines is president of Diners Club of North America. As head of this Citigroup subsidiary, Gaines is responsible for a $30 billion business.[5]

These men and women are just a few of the top black corporate leaders of this nation. They have overcome all the odds and have risen to the very top.

STRIDES IN GOVERNMENT

In addition to holding some of the world's leading positions in business, black Americans are enjoying increasingly key roles at the highest levels of government. For instance, Condoleezza Rice was called the "most influential woman in wartime Washington" during the 2003 war in Iraq.[6]

According to a Newsweek article, Rice is "proud, elegant, fastidious about her appearance (she keeps two mirrors in her office, so she can see her back as well as her front) and utterly unflappable. Rice has Bush's complete confidence; she speaks for the president, and everyone knows it."[7]

The Bush government is racially diverse, with several cabinet positions held by minorities. Even at the highest levels in Washington, D.C., and around the nation, black leadership is continuing to ascend to ever-greater heights. It's an indisputable fact that black Americans are gaining more power as leaders, statesmen and women, and financiers. Blacks are getting wiser, too.

ADVANCING A BLACK POLITICAL AGENDA

I believe we're entering into an era in which blacks will no longer be used as political pawns. As voters, we tend to be loyal, but sometimes to our own detriment. It's time to create our own political agenda and mandate and take it to the political parties instead of continuing to vote from tradition. It's time to vote our conscience, to make the power of our vote work for the black community, instead of allowing political leaders to broker our votes to advance their own agendas.

"In various quarters there are whispers of the need for a black political convention to forge a black political agenda and chart a new direction for black politicians in the twenty-first century," according to Ron Daniels, in an article entitled "Recapturing the Vision and the Spirit of the Gary Convention."[8]

If it happened, it would not be the first time. Thirty years ago, 10,000 black Americans, including elected officials, religious leaders, labor activists, organizers, and politically astute individuals, assembled in Gary, Indiana, for the first National Black Political Convention, convened by Mayor Richard Gordon Hatcher and others. The convention provided analysis of the state of black America, adopted a black political agenda, and launched an independent political organization.[9]

What is our agenda today? I think it's time we came together and figured that out. We need to determine what we truly believe as a community and what we will no longer support as a righteous, holy people. It's time that our community of righteous people stops supporting causes that are unrighteous because our leaders tell us to. We need to begin to use our vote so that everyone in the black community gets a fair shot at equality—educationally, economically, and spiritually.

How will that happen? We have a wealth of undiscovered resources in the power of our leaders. We have leaders whose names we do not know, whose speeches we've never heard. They are not the leaders who speak loudly and often. They do not exist in the media glare or the pursuit of publicity. We need to soberly and wisely seek out leadership that truly represents our needs and community concerns.

More importantly, it's time to hear from God. It's time for our people to say, "Let's see what God has to say to us as a people." And when we hear, we also must act. We must never become the plunder of political charlatans and self-appointed hacks.

For the most part, we're trying to make the government do things for us that we can do for ourselves. If you survey the list of sports and business leaders who have made it to top national positions, there's one thing you'll notice that most, if not all, had in common. They worked hard to make it to the top; no one handed them their positions.

Too many of us continue to labor under the mindset that we need to get somebody else to take care of us. We stopped believing in our own power as individuals long ago. Yet it's that power deep inside each one of us that will make all the difference.

We must start believing in ourselves, and we must start believing in one another.

POLITICIANS AND REAL ANSWERS

There are many good leaders and some very good politicians. Nevertheless, seeking answers to all our problems in the political arena is a tragic mistake. By the time most politicians get into office they have become so compromised and sold out to various agendas that they are no longer free to do what's right.

The answers for the black community and this nation as a whole lie beyond the reach of any particular political agenda. Genuine change will come to this nation when its people decide to base their judgments on the truth of the Bible, not on political agendas.

THE NEW LEADER IS A TRUE LEADER

I'm not convinced that the next generation of leadership for the black community is going to come from the Civil Rights movement. A new leadership is rising up in the black community, but I don't see black leaders politically positioned on the far left as genuinely representing the interests of the black community.

I believe that the true leadership will rise up from the men and women whom God chooses. This new leadership is going to bypass not only the Civil Rights leaders but the religious establishment as well.

There is a distressing leadership void in the black community, as there is in the white and Hispanic communities. The void is particularly glaring when you begin searching for true servant leaders—those who are committed to God first, the people second, and themselves last.

In assessing our leadership, we must ask ourselves: Has that individual been placed into the position by God, or has that person been put into that position by people who like him? Leadership that's not appointed by God will ultimately fail.

Do I see myself as fitting into that leadership void? Not unless God appoints me. The new leadership will be called and appointed by God to make a great difference in the black community for all black people, not just a few. More than anything else, the new black leadership will be focused on seeing the true deliverance of peoples' souls.

ENDNOTES

1. Leland Stein III, "Top 75 Black Athletes and Pioneers of Sports Inclusion," *The Los Angeles Sentinel*; 30 December 1999: www.afrogolf.com/top75blackathletes.html.

2. Deborah Silver, "Minority franchises find wealth of opportunity in city neighborhoods," Urban Lure; 1 September 2000: www.rimag.com.

3. Policy Makers Toolkit; Stories of Entrepreneurs: www.ncoe.org/toolkit/stories_johnson.html.

4. Sam Donnellon, "Robert Johnson proves money is power," *Philadelphia Daily News*; 27 December 2002: www.charlotte.com/mld/charlotte/sports/baketball/4825081.htm.

5. Cora Daniels, "The Most Powerful Black Executives in America," *Fortune*; 22 July 2002.

6. Evan Thomas, "The Quiet Power of Condi Rice," *Newsweek*; 16 December 2002.

7. Ibid., 27.

8. Ron Daniels, "Recapturing the Vision and the Spirit of the Gary Convention," ProfileAfrica; 5 December 2002: www.profileafrica.com/comments3ab.htm.

9. Ibid.

BELIEVING ONCE MORE AND DREAMING AGAIN

He's allowed me to go up to the mountain. And I've looked over.
And I've seen the Promised Land. I may not get there with you.
But I want you to know tonight, that we as a people will get to
the Promised Land. And I'm happy, tonight.
—**Martin Luther King Jr.**

SO MANY YEARS AGO, Martin Luther King Jr. led this nation's blacks across a harsh wilderness and placed within its heart the seed of a dream. Just as the biblical Moses never entered the Promised Land, this twentieth century Moses never went in either. But he showed us the way. Some of us journeyed in the wilderness, suffered the heat, stumbled, stood back up, and dared to dream the dream. Many of us who have wandered will enter in.

More importantly, I'm convinced that there is a generation of young black men and women who never had to experience the heat of the desert sun or the painful, parched throbbing of thirst. That generation is growing up, maturing, learning wisdom and knowledge, and gaining favor with God and man. This

169

young, intelligent leadership will shake up the kingdoms of men and turn the nation on its heels.

I, Too, Have a Dream

Dr. King looked over into the good land and saw the vision, and he spoke about it. He gave us his assurance that we, too, would see it. We would go in.

The Israelites grieved the loss of Moses in the wilderness, and we have grieved the loss of King. When the Israelites arose from their grieving, they rubbed their eyes and started searching for their new leaders. They started asking who now would take them in.

Today's black community must ask the same question. What will the new leadership look like? Now that Moses—King—is dead, who will take us into the Promised Land?

The next generation of leadership will look like Abraham, Isaac, Moses, and the prophets of old. They will be leaders who are God-appointed, not self-appointed or man-appointed. This new leadership will speak what God has called them to speak, even if doing so exacts a cost of death.

The next generation of leadership will look like martyrs such as Dr. King and others. They will resemble the Old Testament prophets and the New Testament apostles, such as Peter, Paul, and James. They will proclaim what God tells them, even when it places them in danger.

The new leadership will be appointed solely by the God of Abraham, Isaac, and Jacob. They won't be voted into power, and they won't come with a political agenda. They will preach the message that God has placed within them, and their words will shake the foundations of the religious and political establishments. Eventually, even the politicians and religious leaders who

170

hate them and oppose them will receive their words. When that occurs, change will come.

A JOSHUA GENERATION

This leadership will have a heart burning to benefit God's people. They will be servant leaders, and the purity of their lifestyles will shame corrupt leaders. Corrupt leaders will be forced to see that they've been man-pleasers, self-indulgent, and overly concerned with building their own kingdoms and advancing their own agendas.

The power of these new leaders will cause those from every culture to change their personal priorities and become committed to building up God's people.

I believe that this Joshua generation of leadership is being prepared right now. Older leaders will marvel at their intelligence and wonder where it came from. It will be apparent that they received it from God Himself.

Right now these kids are being trained to disregard what others think about them. Some are former gang members; some have been in jail. Many have been down and out. But God is ready to raise them up, and when that happens we'll hear the voice of God speaking through their lives, calling us out of racism, hatred, confusion, and division into the brotherhood of man—the Promised Land of the Messiah.

BIBLIOGRAPHY

Anderson, Claud, Ed. D. *Black Labor White Wealth.* Bethesda, MD: PowerNomics Corporation of America, 1994.

_____. *Dirty Little Secrets.* Bethesda, MD: PowerNomics Corporation of America, 1997.

Archer, Jules. *They Had a Dream.* New York: Viking, 1993.

Beckner, Christine. *100 Black Americans Who Shaped History.* San Francisco: A Bluewood Book, 1995.

Brooks, Roy L. *Integration or Separation?* Cambridge, MA: Harvard University Press, 1996.

Garrow, David J. *Bearing the Cross, Martin Luther King, Jr., and the Southern Christian Leadership Conference.* New York: William Morrow and Company, Inc., 1986.

Haskins, Jim. *I Have a Dream.* Brookfield, CT: The Millbrook Press, 1992.

Jacoby, Tamar. *Someone Else's House.* New York: Basic Books, Perseus Books Group, 1998.

King, Coretta Scott. *The Martin Luther King, Jr. Companion.* New York: St. Martin's Press, 1963.

King, Martin Luther Jr. *A Call to Conscience.* Edited by Clayborne Carson, Kris Shepard. New York: Warner Books, 2001.

_____. *A Knock at Midnight.* Edited by Clayborne Carson, Peter Holloran. New York: Warner Books, 1998.

_____ . *The Triumph of Conscience.* San Francisco: Harper & Row Publishers, 1967.

_____ . *Why We Can't Wait.* New York: Signet Classic, 1963.

Osthaus, Carl R. *Freedmen, Philanthropy, and Fraud.* Urbana, IL: University of Illinois Press, 1976.

Reese, Ed. *Blacks Used of God.* Lake Wales, FL: Reese Religious Research, n.d.

Ryun, Jim. *Heroes Among Us.* Shippensburg, PA: Destiny Image, 2002.

Smith, Jessie Carney. *Black Firsts.* Detroit, MI: Visible Ink, 1994.

Timmerman, Kenneth R. *Shakedown.* Washington, DC: Regnery Publishing, Inc., 2002.